TABLE OF CONTENTS

TRAVIS PICKING

BY ANDREW DUBROCK

PLAYBACK+
Speed Pitch Balance Loop

To access audio visit:
www.halleonard.com/mylibrary

Enter Code
1582-9465-3487-8829

ISBN 978-1-4234-9435-5

HAL•LEONARD® CORPORATION
7777 W. BLUEMOUND RD. P.O. BOX 13819 MILWAUKEE, WI 53213

In Australia Contact:
Hal Leonard Australia Pty. Ltd.
4 Lentara Court
Cheltenham, Victoria, 3192 Australia
Email: ausadmin@halleonard.com.au

Visit Hal Leonard Online at
www.halleonard.com

PREFACE

Travis picking derives its name from a single man—Merle Travis—and his unique method of fingerpicking the guitar. But over the years, the term has broadened to encompass more than just one brilliant picker's style.

It's important to note that Travis didn't come up with this technique entirely on his own; some of his contemporaries played in this style, and Travis was simply the one to popularize the technique in the late 1930s, when he became a country music star. Since then, his name has always been associated with it.

The foundation of Travis picking revolves around the combination of *alternate-bass fingerpicking* and *syncopated melodies*. And, while Travis and his contemporaries were perfecting the technique in Tennessee, pickers across other styes—like folk and country-blues pickers—were integrating similar techniques into their playing.

By the 1960s, popular singer/songwriters like Simon & Garfunkel were using syncopated alternate-bass fingerpicking patterns to accompany themselves. While these songs generally used more basic patterns than Travis would have played, guitar teachers taught these patterns as "Travis picking" to their students—thus expanding the definition of *Travis picking* to include not only Travis's own style, but also styles of playing that were inspired by Travis.

This book studies all of these types of picking in a progressive fashion—starting with the alternate-bass accompaniment patterns, followed by the melodic alternate-bass picking often affiliated with country-blues or folk pickers (which might not always be referred to as *Travis picking*), and finishing with the type of picking Travis himself played. They're all valuable tools to have in your guitar-playing bag, and there's a natural progression in difficulty from one to the next.

Thanks to Jeff Schroedl and Hal Leonard for bringing you this guide to *Travis Picking*.

—Andrew DuBrock

ABOUT THE AUTHOR

Andrew DuBrock is an independent music consultant who lives in Portland, Oregon. He has worked as an editor, transcriber, engraver, and author for Hal Leonard, and served as Music Editor for *Acoustic Guitar*, *Strings*, and *Play Guitar!* magazines for seven years. A sampling of his instructional works include *Total Acoustic Guitar*, *Lennon and McCartney for Acoustic Guitar* (DVD), and *Rock/Pop Guitar Songs for Dummies*. His independent acoustic pop-rock CD, *DuBrock*, can be found at *dubrock.net* and *cdbaby.com*.

To see more books and articles by Andrew DuBrock, or if you have comments or questions about this book, visit *andrewdubrock.com*.

INTRODUCTION

Travis picking got its name from Merle Travis, but it could have easily been called a number of other things—like "Everly picking" or "Rager picking," for the two other men who helped form the style. Those two men, Ike Everly and Mose Rager, were Kentucky pickers who played around the Muhlenberg County area—a part of Kentucky known for its coal mining (and which also inspired John Prine's song "Paradise"—a song set around a Muhlenberg County town that later became a coal mine). Everly and Rager incorporated the use of a *thumbpick* and *palm-muting* techniques they learned from other local pickers like Kennedy Jones, Jim Mason, and Amos Johnson, and wove those elements into their own style of "thumbpicking." Travis loved the style and picked it up as well—eventually becoming a friend and collaborator with Everly and Rager.

When Travis later became a regular performer on Cincinnati's WLW radio station, this type of picking was broadcast to a much wider audience, and his name became attached to the style. (Incidentally, Everly's name also became famous when his two sons formed a duo called the "Everly Brothers.") A young Chet Atkins heard Travis on the radio and couldn't believe it was just one guitar. Atkins would take Travis's picking style to an even larger audience when he became a prominent Nashville guitarist and producer. Since then, the term "Travis picking" has broadened even further to incorporate syncopated alternate-bass accompaniment patterns that were inspired by Travis's style and used by pop and rock acts of the latter 20th century. This book will take a look at all of these types of picking—starting with the popular accompaniment picking patterns and progressively building towards the final section, which features several chapters of Travis-style picking based on Merle Travis's and Chet Atkins' own playing.

GUITARS AND FINGERPICKS

Travis picking works equally well on acoustic *and* electric guitars. While Merle Travis was often seen with a large-bodied acoustic guitar or a semi-hollowbody electric guitar, other types—like smaller acoustic guitars and even solidbody electrics—will work fine for this technique. Use the equipment you have, and if you want to recreate a particular artist's sound, then you can seek out a guitar similar to what that artist used.

All types of Travis picking use the thumb and one or more fingers to pluck the strings, but it's your choice as to whether you use a thumbpick and/or fingerpicks, bare fingers, or fingernails. Fingernails and (especially) fingerpicks tend to provide a brighter, louder sound, while fingers tend to provide a warmer, mellower sound. Both Merle Travis and Chet Atkins often used a thumbpick without fingerpicks.

Tuning Notes

TRACK 1

SECTION I
ACCOMPANIMENT PATTERNS

This section builds your Travis picking foundation by studying accompaniment Travis-picking patterns popularized by pop acts and taught by guitar teachers in the modern era. While this style of fingerpicking is not the way Merle Travis played, it's a popular offshoot inspired by his playing and a great method for accompanying yourself! Just as importantly, this type of accompaniment serves as a springboard to help give you the techniques to play more like Travis himself did, and we'll explore his playing in the third section of this book (Advanced Travis Picking).

CHAPTER 1:
ALTERNATE-BASS FINGERPICKING

Alternate-bass fingerpicking is the foundation for all Travis-based fingerpicking. As its name implies, this technique alternates between two or more strings to play bass notes. Some simple fingerpicking patterns roll across the strings with the thumb (*p*, in the notation) playing held notes, and the index (*i*), middle (*m*), and ring (*a*) fingers assigned to their own strings (below, left). Other fingerpicking patterns might park the thumb on one string for the bass notes, again assigning the thumb and fingers to their own strings (below, middle). Alternate-bass fingerpicking uses your thumb to alternate between different strings; your thumb plays all the bass notes, while your fingers play accompaniment patterns or melodies on the top strings (below, right).

TRACK 2

Simple Fingerpicking Pattern:

Monotonic Bass Fingerpicking Pattern:

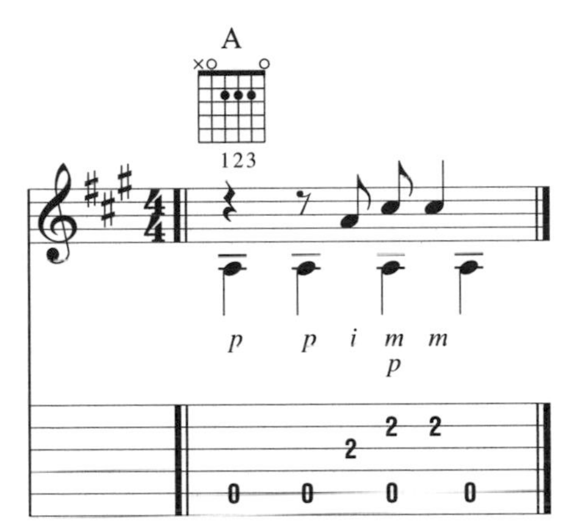

Alternate-Bass Fingerpicking (Travis Picking):

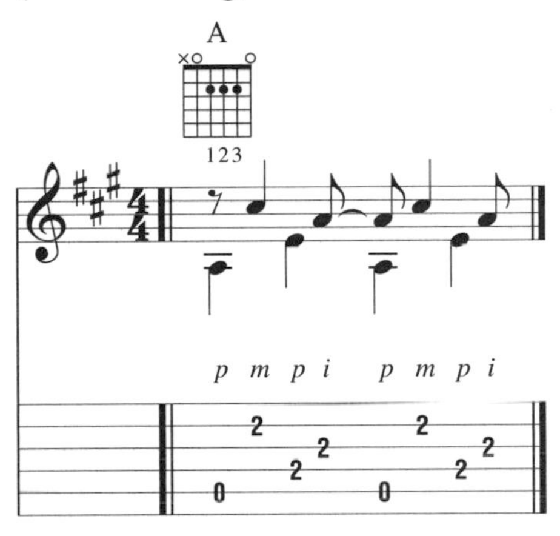

Don't worry if you have trouble playing any of the above examples; they're here just to show you how Travis picking looks compared to several other styles of fingerpicking. If you *can* already play these patterns—great!—you're ahead of the game.

For those of you who can't immediately play the above Travis-picking pattern, let's work up to it. As we begin, it's helpful to slow things down and break things apart, so let's first get the thumb going on its own. Here's the thumb part of our example by itself:

TRACK 3

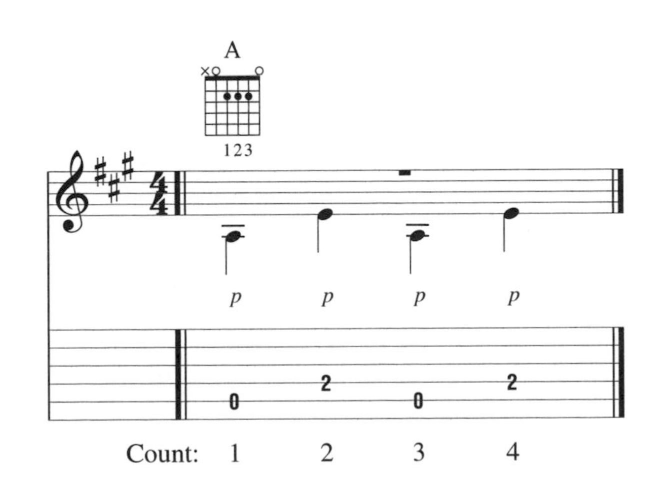

Count: 1 2 3 4

Next, gradually add the fingers. Start by adding your index finger on the "&" of beat 1. Count along, using *eighth-note subdivisions* ("1–&, 2–&, 3–&, 4–&"), and slow it down to the point where you can repeat the measure without slowing down when you play the note with your index finger. As you get the hang of it, you can gradually speed up.

TRACK 3
(0:08)

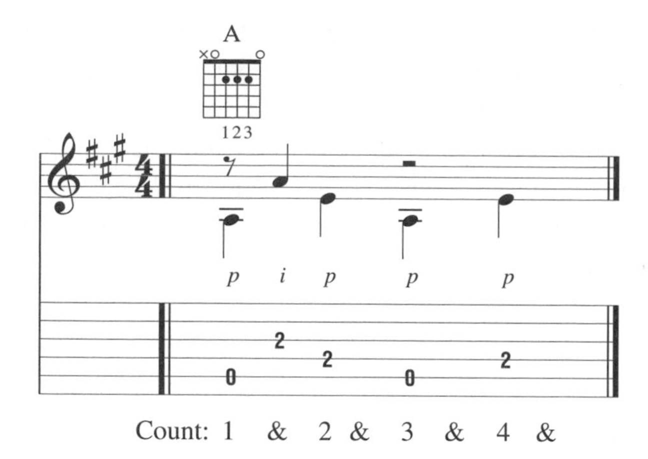

Once you have this down, try alternating *every* bass note with your index finger, like this:

TRACK 3
(0:17)

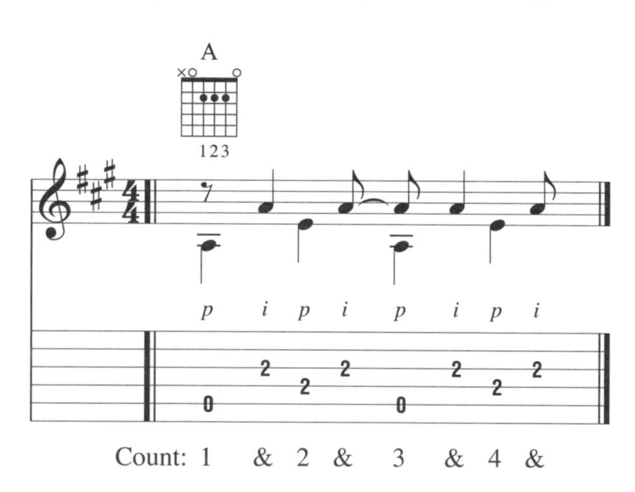

Now let's use our middle finger, instead of our index finger.

TRACK 4

If you need to, slow this down to get it under your fingers and remember that you can always cut back to one note per measure with your middle finger—just as we did with our index finger.

Once you have these two patterns down, try mixing them together by alternating between your middle and index fingers, like this:

TRACK 4
(0:09)

If you made it through the last example, congratulations! You're playing the basic Travis-picking pattern and you can already play many songs with just this pattern. For instance, notice how close the following example is to the picking pattern and sound of Kansas's "Dust in the Wind."

TRACK 5

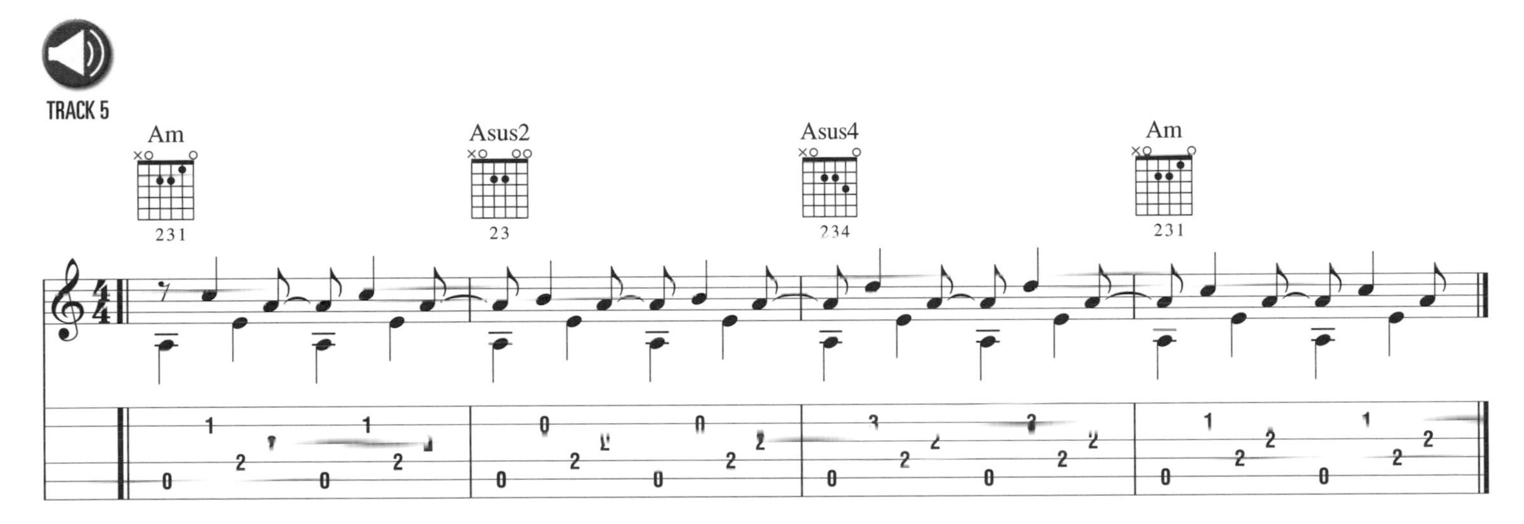

ADDING THE RING FINGER

Many guitarists play these patterns exclusively using their index and middle fingers. You can play countless songs this way, but you can play many more patterns if you can add your ring finger whenever you want to. Let's warm your ring finger up by playing it on every *offbeat* (the eighth-note "&s").

TRACK 6

Now try integrating it with the other fingers in the following pattern:

TRACK 6
(0:08)

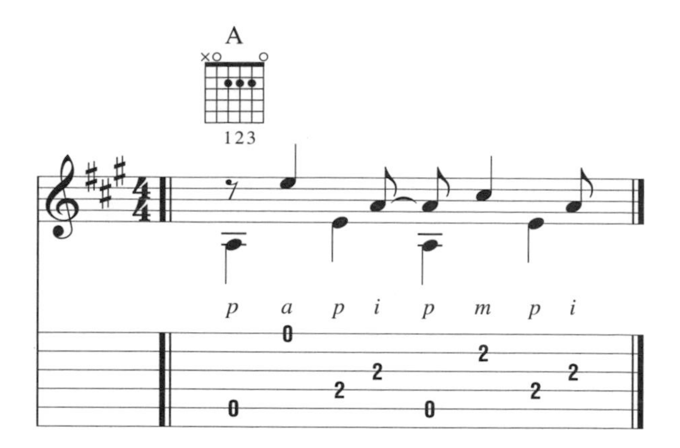

Adding this finger to your picking patterns allows you to easily cover more strings. While plenty of people don't use this finger, often playing everything with just the one pattern we learned, there are countless players who *do* use the ring finger to play many different patterns and variations. For instance, without that ring finger, you wouldn't get the characteristic high G note of this Am7 chord shape—a shape used in the Beatles' song "Julia" and played with a similar pattern.

TRACK 7

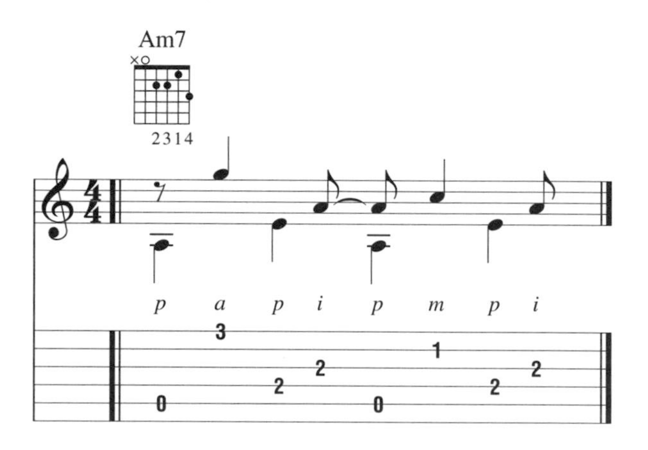

TRAVIS PICKING ANY CHORD

So far, we've only played patterns with versions of A chords, but you can use the very same A chord patterns for any chord with a root note on the fifth string (the *root* is usually the lowest note of any standard chord and shares the same letter name as the chord). Here's how it sounds using a C chord:

TRACK 8

Notice how the C chord accompaniment sounds a little different. That's because you're playing the 3rd of the C chord (the note E) on the fourth string, instead of the 5th of the chord, like you do over the A chord (that same E note is the 5th of an A chord). Try it over other chords that have a root on the fifth string, like B7:

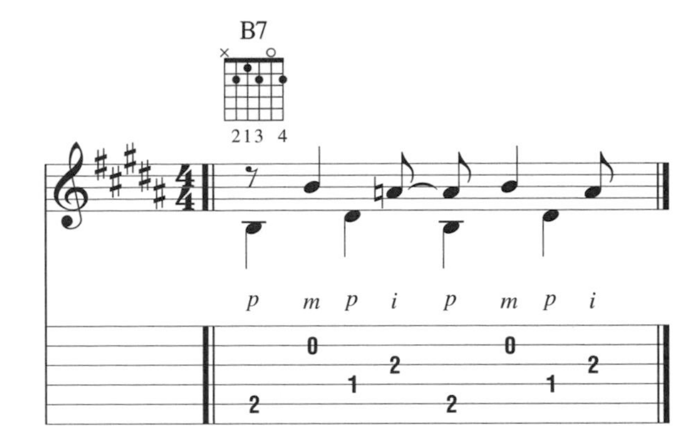

Of course, you can also use it with any barre-chord shape that has a root on the fifth string, like these B and B7 barre chords:

Now, to apply that concept to a D chord, or any chord with the root on the *fourth* string, simply move your fingers up a string so your thumb rests on the fourth string—rocking back and forth between the fourth and third strings—and your index and middle fingers are parked on the second and first strings, respectively. This bumps your ring finger off the fretboard, but you won't need that finger since a D chord only covers four strings.

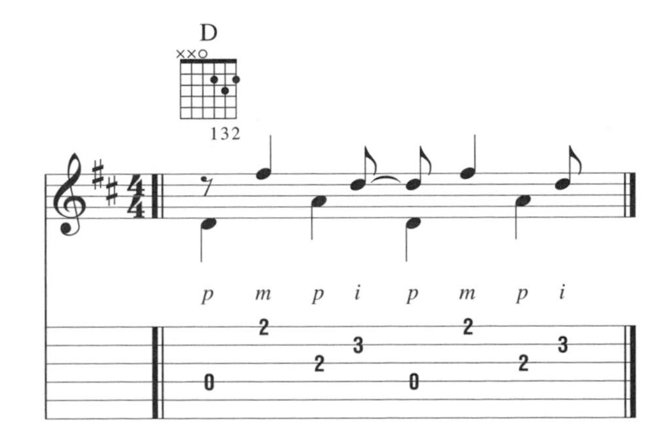

Now that we know patterns that use more than one string set, it's a good idea to practice moving between these patterns so you can change chords more quickly and easily. Let's try this out with the A–D chord change below.

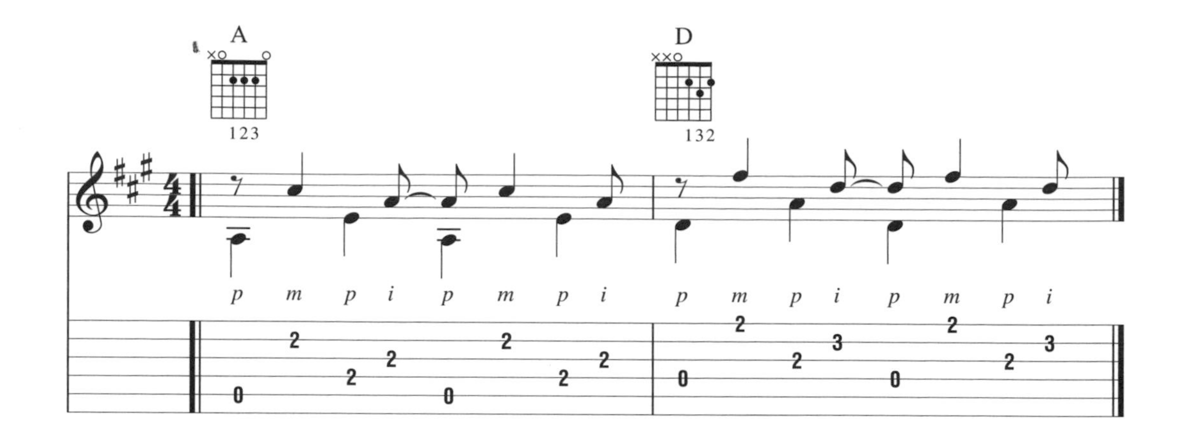

For chords that have a root on the sixth string, start with your fingers in position for your A chord and move *only your thumb* down to the sixth string; your index, middle, and ring fingers will stick to the top three strings. While your thumb *could* rock between the sixth and fifth strings, most fingerpickers actually skip the fifth string, alternating between the sixth and fourth strings with their thumb, like this:

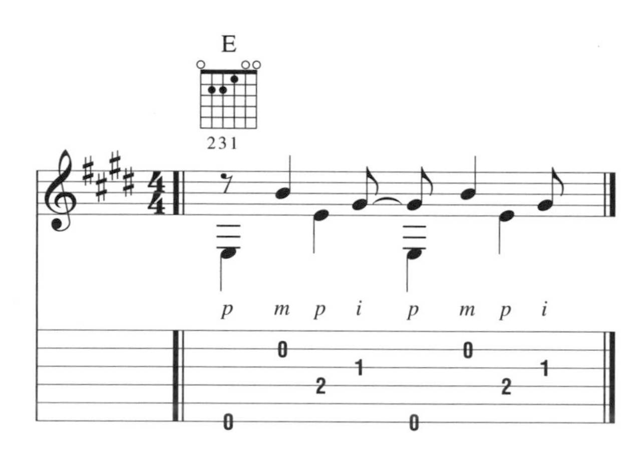

This works for any chord with a root on the sixth string, like this G chord:

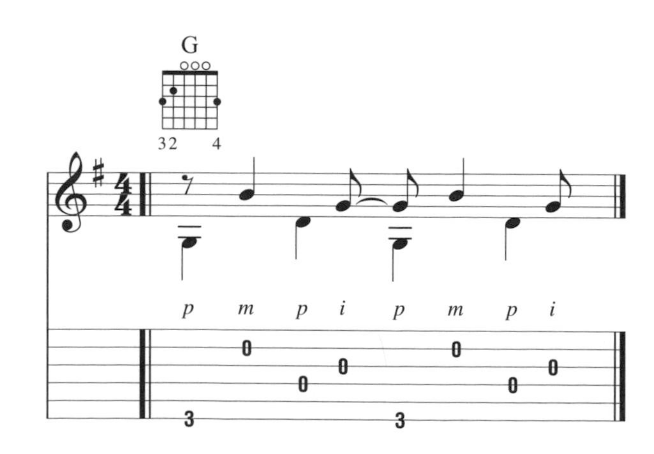

Again, now that we've learned our pattern with another string set, it's a good idea to practice moving between different sets of strings so you can change chords within songs more quickly and fluidly. This G–Am–C–D chord progression uses all three string sets we've learned, integrating chords with roots on the sixth, fifth, and fourth strings.

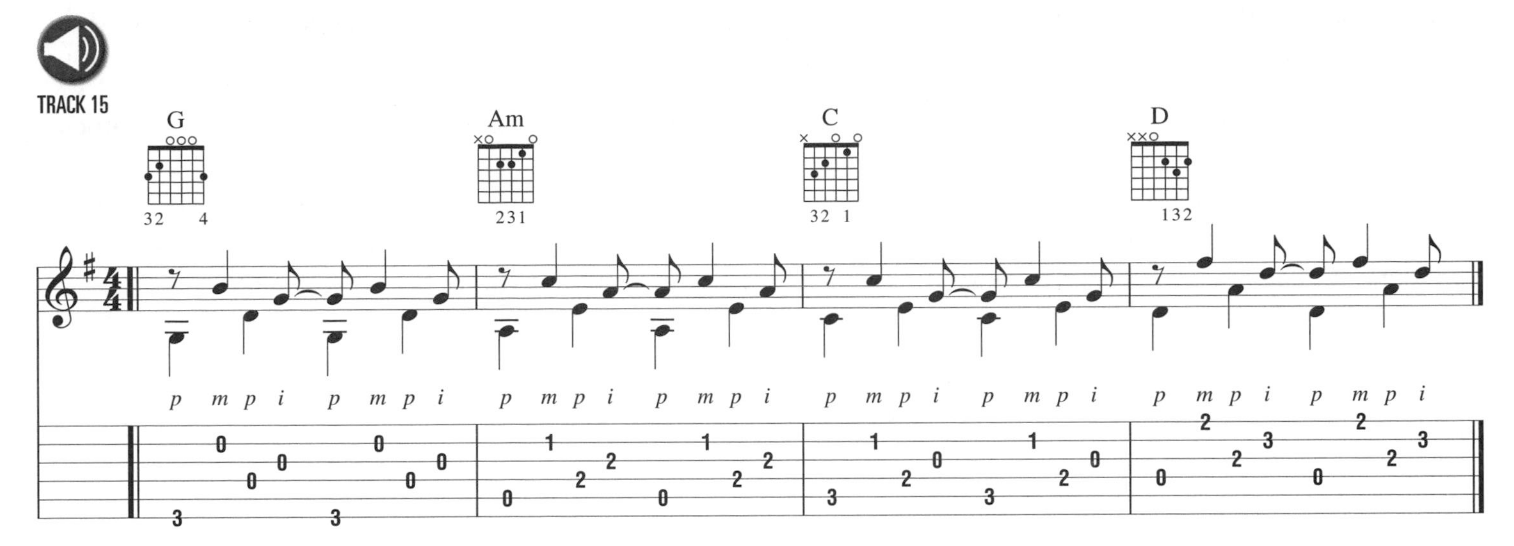

Remember that you can play barre chords this way as well. Once you apply this technique to barre chords with their root on the sixth string—like the F and Fm chords here—you've got the tools to Travis pick nearly any chord type, anywhere on the neck (combining root-position chords with barre chord shapes that have their roots on either the fifth or sixth strings):

BREAK THE RULES!

Remember that rules were meant to be broken! For instance, the following pattern uses your thumb on the sixth and fifth strings (which we avoided a moment ago) and shifts your fingers down one string to play the fourth and third strings.

SWEET SUNNY SOUTH

Now that we can Travis pick many different chords, let's try playing them in a complete song. The traditional tune "Sweet Sunny South" is a great song for this type of Travis picking. Joan Baez is one of many people who played this song, and she performed the tune at the famous Woodstock concert in 1969.

Playing through songs is a great way to practice moving the picking pattern from one set of strings to another—something we've practiced only a little bit so far. Notice how the transitions from G to C (measures 9–10 and 12–13) or from C back to G (measures 11–12 and 13–14) are much easier than the transitions from G to D (measures 14–15 and 17–18) or from D back to G (measures 16–17 and 18–19). That's because only your thumb switches strings between the C and G chords, whereas you'll need to move the whole formation up or down to move between G and D.

TRACK 18

SWEET SUNNY SOUTH

Traditional, arranged by Andrew DuBrock

C
G
9
take me home
where the mock - ing birds
C
G
D
13
sing me to rest
ev-'ry night.
Oh,
G
D
G
17
why was I tempt - ed to roam?

If you have trouble with any of these moves, isolate those measures of the piece, repeat them at a slow speed until you have them under your fingers, then gradually speed them up to performance tempo:

TRACK 19

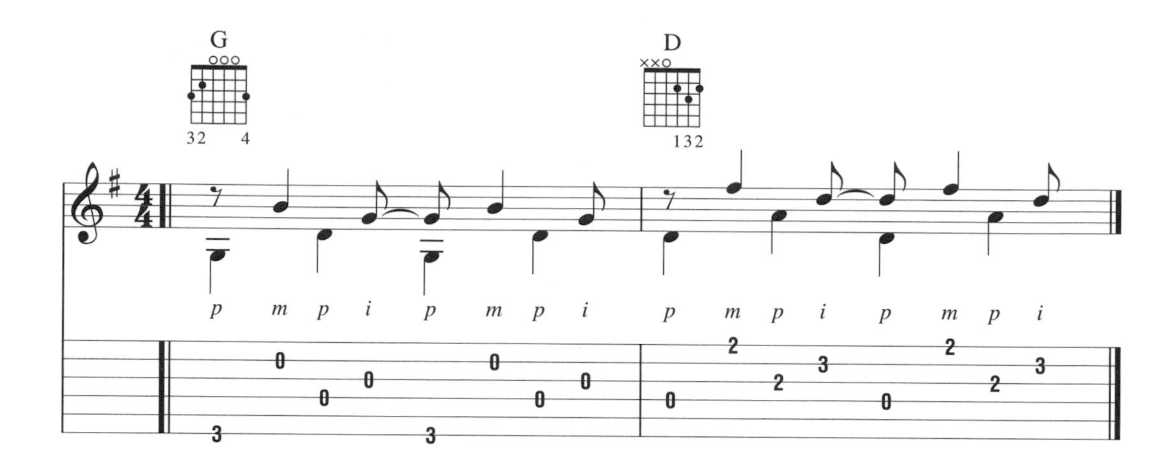

Practice these picking patterns on other songs you know and make sure to isolate, slow down, and repeat any chord changes that cause you trouble. This is a great way to practice moving between chords, since you're playing songs instead of simply running through exercises.

CHAPTER 2:
THICKENING THE BASS AND ADDING THE PINCH

You can already play many songs with your three- and four-finger Travis picking patterns, but there are plenty of ways you can embellish them to give your tunes more variety. In this chapter, we'll expand the bass by alternating between *three* strings, and we'll also add pinches to our playing. For more on bass and *pinches* (plucking notes with the thumb and fingers simultaneously), read on.

THREE-STRING BASS

So far, our Travis-picking patterns have used a two-note bass pattern that rocks between the lowest note of a chord and the next highest string, like this:

TRACK 20

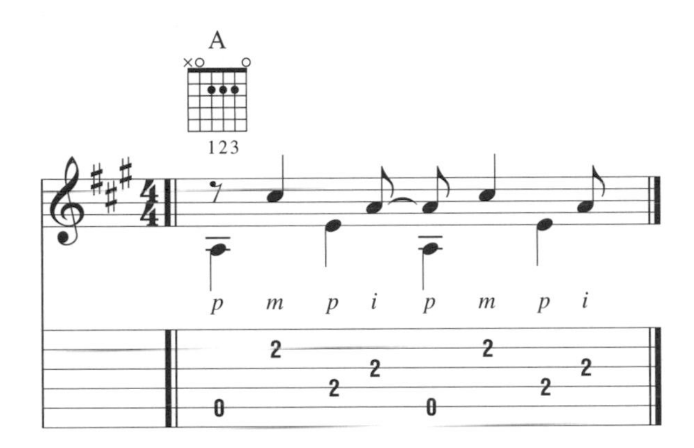

To expand our bass, we need to look at the thumb part as a four-note pattern instead of a two-note pattern, then add that extra string as the *third* note. For most chords—like the A shown here—that means jumping down to the string *below* the lowest note in the chord. First, let's try this out with just the thumb:

TRACK 20
(0:07)

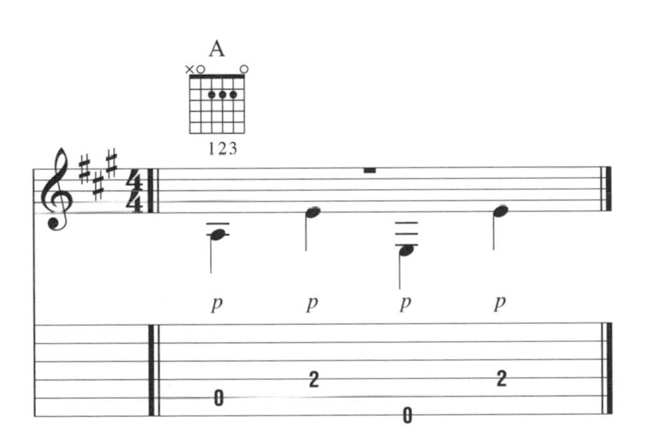

Now try adding the fingers:

TRACK 20
(0:15)

That low E string can sometimes muddy things up a bit. Whenever you find this to be the case, you can always reach over the neck with your fret-hand thumb to briefly mute the note while playing the open fifth string.

Playing this low string at all might seem strange—we don't usually play the string *below* the lowest note in a chord. For an A chord, this works fine because that open E string is actually a note in the chord, but for many other chords, this will take some adjustment because the lower open string might not be a note that works with the chord we're playing. Let's try this with a C chord to see how it works:

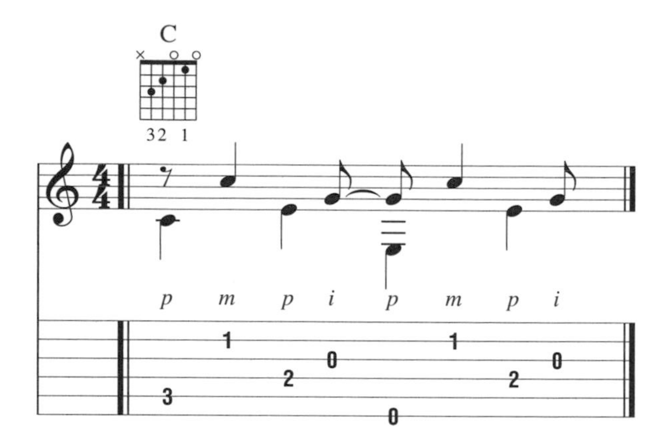

This actually sounds OK because the low E string is still a note in the C chord, but playing it this way often sounds a bit muddy, so most people play the C chord by fretting the 3rd-fret G note on the lowest string. There are two ways you can fret this note: you can either readjust your fret-hand fingers to play it using your ring finger, *or* you could rock back and forth between the fifth and sixth strings with your ring finger, fretting the proper bass note just before you pluck it. The "rocking" method might take some getting used to, but it's the more common way to play the chord and provides natural string damping because your ring finger is only playing one bass note at a time. (Sometimes when two bass notes ring together, it creates that muddy sound we don't like; that's why *damping* is helpful.)

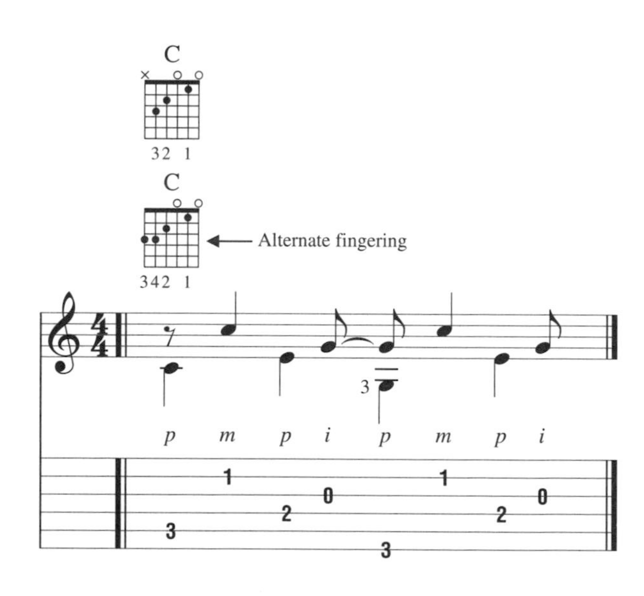

Does the above example sound familiar? This pattern, over a C chord, is a common sound, and you might recognize it from tunes like Simon & Garfunkel's "The Boxer."

Now let's try this with a B7 chord. That low E string won't work with this chord (try it and you'll see!), but the 2nd-fret F♯ note *will* work since it's part of a B7 chord. The B7 chord requires all four fingers, so to play this pattern, you'll need to rock between the 2nd-fret notes on the bottom two strings with your middle finger.

TRACK 22

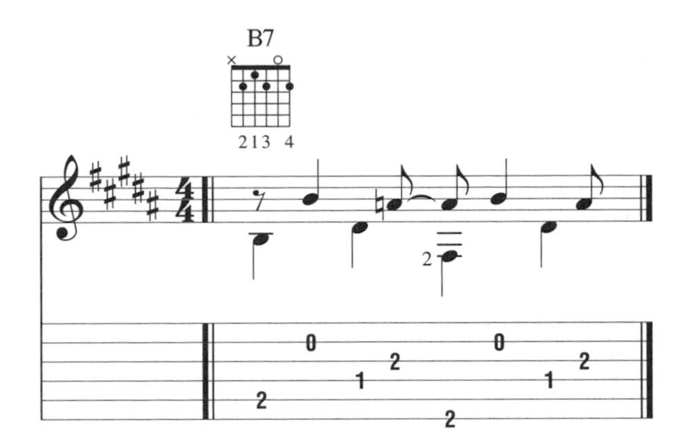

To play this pattern using barre chords with a root on the fifth string, you'll need one small adjustment: extend that index-finger barre across all six strings so it covers the lowest string as well. Then you can play any barre-chord shape with its root on the fifth string, like this C7 chord:

TRACK 23

For the few rhythm chords that have their lowest note on the fourth string—like D—go down to the fifth string for the bass note on beat 3. With a D chord, that open A string works fine, since A is part of a D chord:

TRACK 24

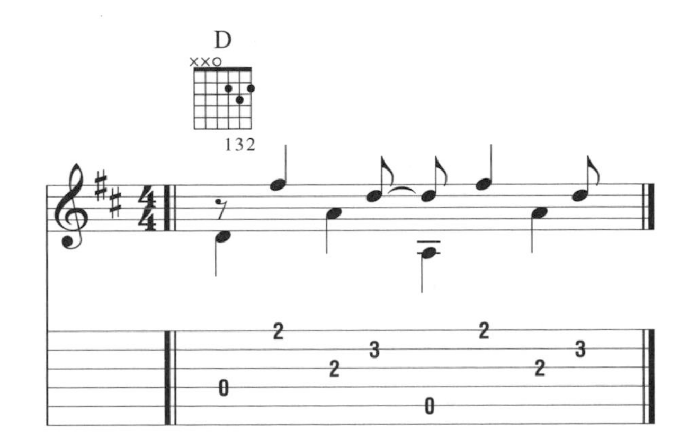

When we apply our three-string bass pattern to six-string chords, we don't have a lower string to pick like we do with other chords, so we'll have to add that bass note somewhere else. Since our pattern for these types of chords usually alternates between the sixth and fourth strings, we'll use the fifth string as the added bass note. This is how it sounds for an E chord:

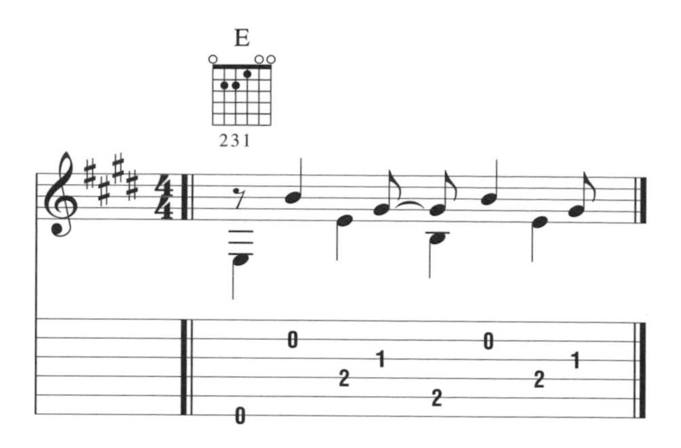

Sixth-string barre chords don't require any adjustment. Simply playing the same pattern as the previous E chord will work for any barre chord, like this F♯7 chord:

THE PINCH

Whenever you play a note with your finger simultaneously with a thumbpicked bass note, you're playing a *pinch*. Let's try this out with an A chord, adding a pinch on the first beat. (We'll go back to alternating between just two strings for the bass notes so we're not integrating too many things at once. But you can practice any of these patterns with a three-string bass pattern, as well.)

This is just one small alteration to our pattern, but notice how it makes things sound very different. The two pinched notes create a bit of a natural accent, but by moving that middle-finger note ahead by an eighth note, it also creates an eighth-note space between the thumbpicked notes on beats 1 and 2—a bit of a pause. In chapter 1, we saw a Travis-picking pattern that was similar to Kansas's hit "Dust in the Wind," but notice how, when we add a pinch to that chord progression, it sounds even more similar:

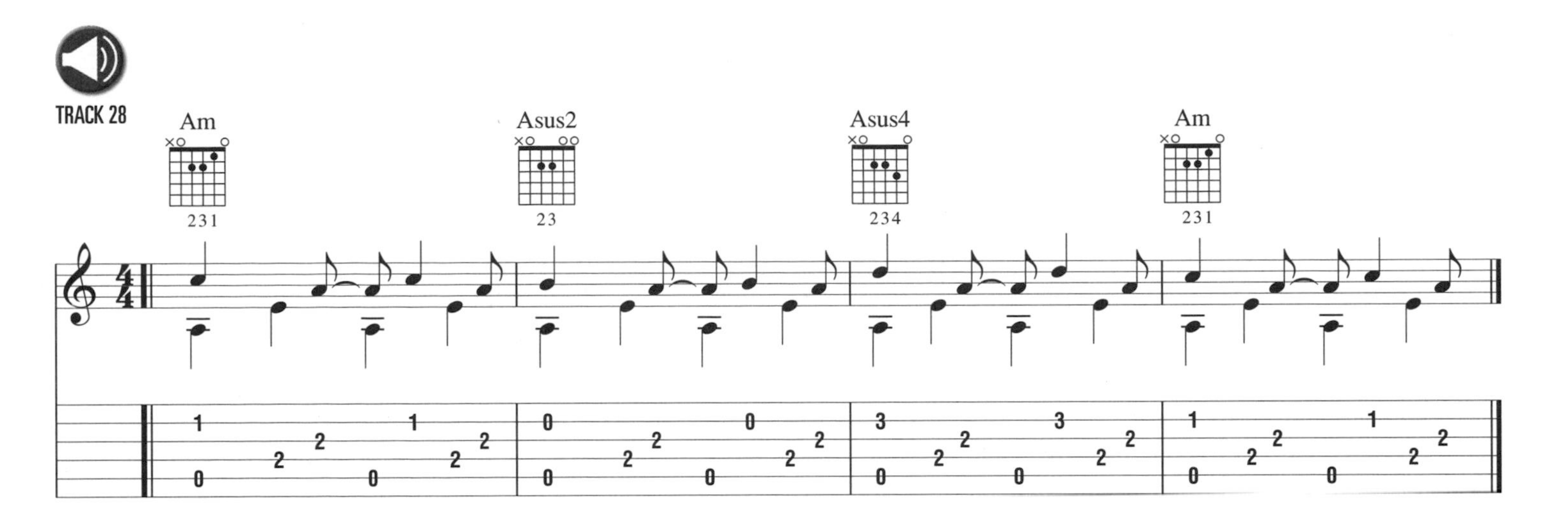

You can use any of your fingers to play a pinch. Let's try it now with our ring finger.

Here's a pinch with our index finger:

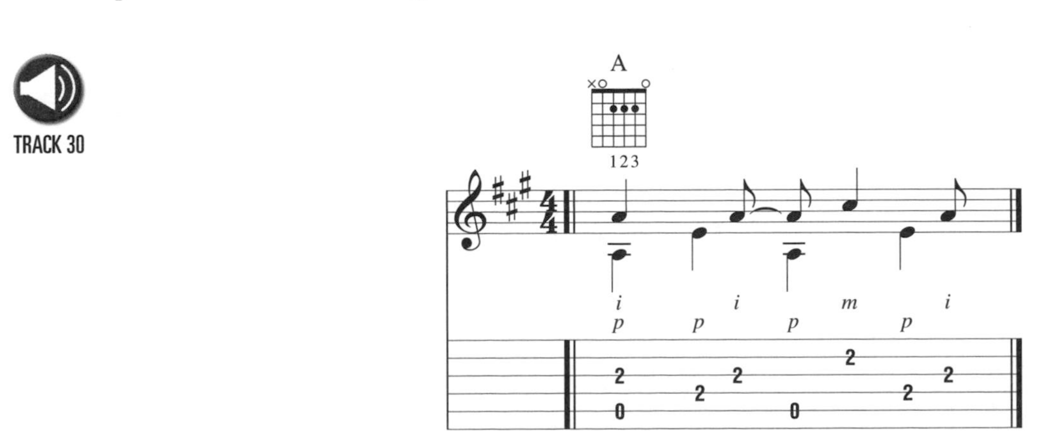

You'll notice how this pattern's a bit more difficult on the repeat because your index finger has to quickly play two notes in a row. For a smoother pattern, let's modify it so as to leave out the final eighth note of the measure; now our index finger has plenty of time to prepare for the pinch when we repeat the pattern:

TRACK 30
(0:08)

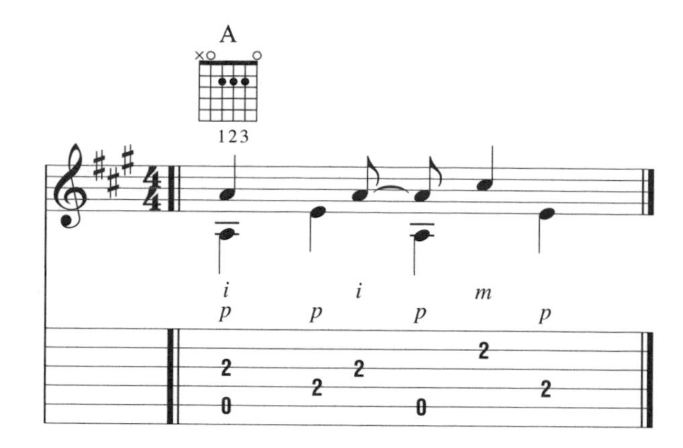

Of course, you can add a pinch to your Travis-picking pattern for any chord type—whether it has its lowest note on the fourth, fifth, or sixth string. Here's a pinch using a D chord. Notice how this one sounds a bit like the Beatles' song "Dear Prudence":

TRACK 31

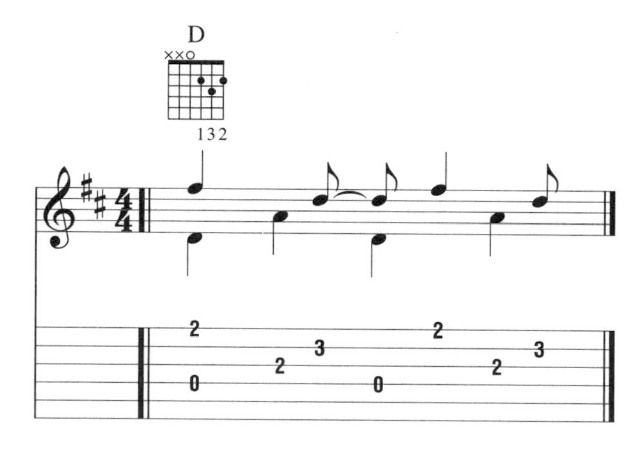

And here's a pinch pattern using an E chord. We'll alternate between E and A chords here to start getting you comfortable with pinching chords with root notes on different strings. Notice that the last eighth note of each measure is an open string; this happens because the picking hand is playing a note while the fretting hand is moving to grab the next chord.

TRACK 32

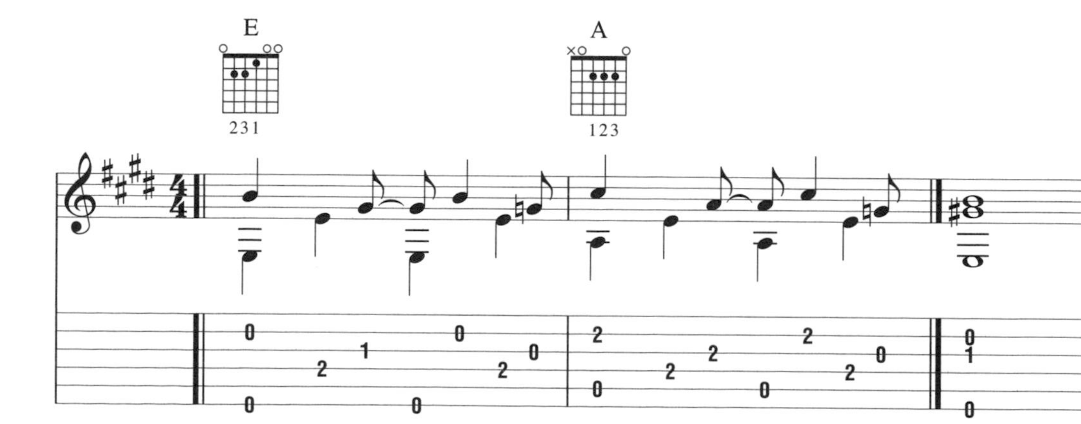

And here are some pinches played with fifth- and sixth-string barre chords.

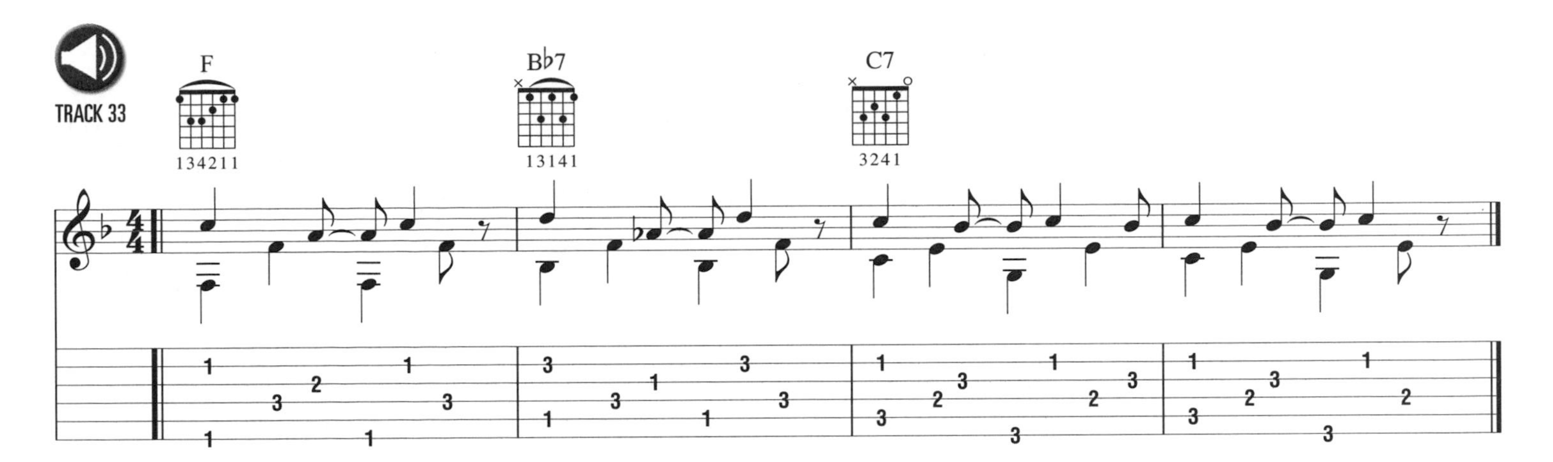

Well, technically, that C7 isn't a barre chord, but it's a nice position to use with this pattern, so I slipped it in there! Notice how I've left out the last eighth note of measures 1, 2, and 4 to give our hands a little more time to get into formation for the coming chord. Of course, you can continue to pick here, but you'll probably hit a ghost note or an open string as your fret-hand fingers are making their way from one chord to the next.

Try Starting with Different Bass Notes

All of the picking patterns start with your thumb playing the root note for its first bass note, but other bass notes can work for the first note, as well. For instance, here's an Em chord that starts by playing the 5th in the bass (the B note on the fifth string), but then rocks between the fourth and sixth strings:

If this sounds familiar, it's because this chord and picking pattern is similar to one John Lennon used in the Beatles' song "Julia." Patterns like this are often used in context with other chords that use the same pattern, and when the same pattern is played with the other chords, the root note is first. For instance, here's a C–Em chord progression using this picking pattern. Note how we're using the same picking pattern for both chords, but the C chord starts with its root note, while the Em chord starts with its 5th.

SWEET SUNNY SOUTH

Let's finish things off by dressing up the song "Sweet Sunny South" from chapter 1 to see how our new tricks—the pinches and three-string bass—can spice this tune up. As you can see, the opening measures are unchanged (I liked the rolling feel of pinchless picking and two-string bass here). But notice how, in measure 5, I added a three-string bass move just before the chord change to D because I liked the way it gave a feeling of forward momentum to the D chord. You'll see the same thing happen in measure 9 to help the transition from G to C. In measures 14 and 17, however, I've kept the two-string bass movement under the G chord; the chord movement seemed quick enough that it didn't need any extra motion in the bass. For all of the C chords, I opted for the three-string bass because I like the way it sounded on that chord.

You'll also notice that, for the D chord in measures 6–7, there's not much vocal happening, so I added pinches and three-string bass to fill in and create a little interest. You'll see the same thing during the C chord in measures 10–11 and the D chord in measures 15–16—two areas where the vocal line pauses again.

SWEET SUNNY SOUTH

Traditional, arranged by Andrew DuBrock

C
G
9
take me home
where the mock - ing birds

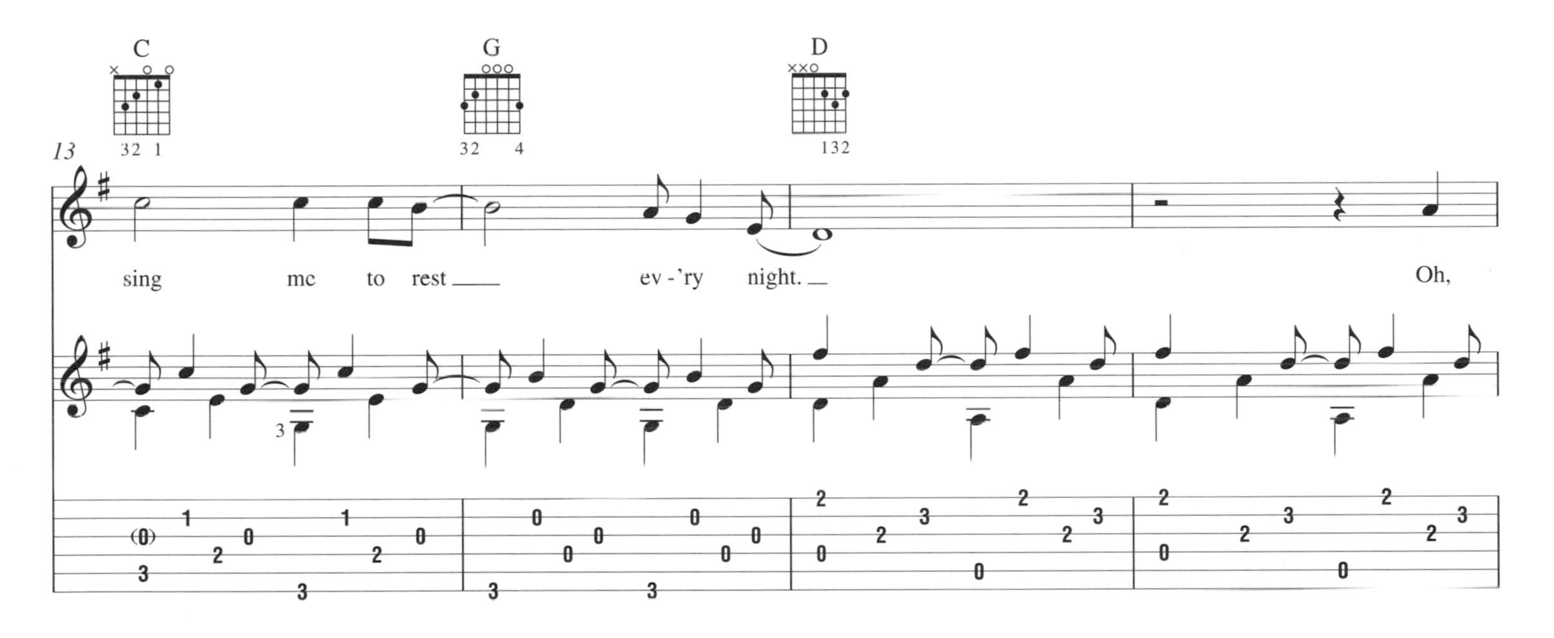
C
G
D
13
sing me to rest
ev - 'ry night.
Oh,

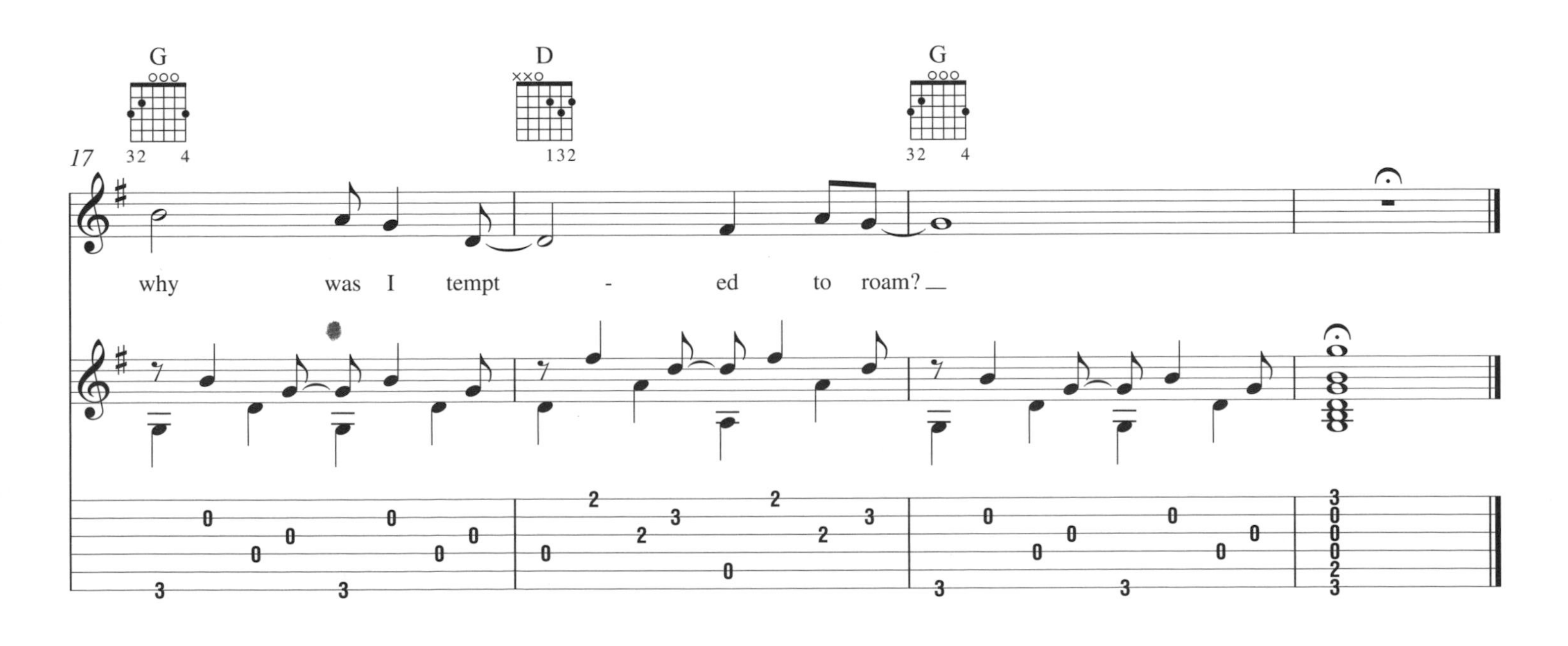
G
D
G
17
why was I tempt - ed to roam?

CHAPTER 3:
MOVING BASS LINES AND PICKING VARIATIONS

At this point, you have the tools to create quite a variety of Travis-picking accompaniments. When you vary each of these patterns, a whole new world of picking opens up. In this chapter, we'll look at one more technique: how you can add *moving bass lines* to your Travis-picking patterns. Then we'll explore how you can vary all of these techniques to create a nearly limitless number of Travis-picking patterns and accompaniments.

MOVING BASS LINES

When we played "Sweet Sunny South" in the last chapter, we added three-string bass lines to our G chord in several places, just before moving to another chord. That's because bass motion can often help chords move more smoothly into other chords; when it works, it usually sounds better. To see and hear the difference, first play this example—two measures of G, followed by two measures of C:

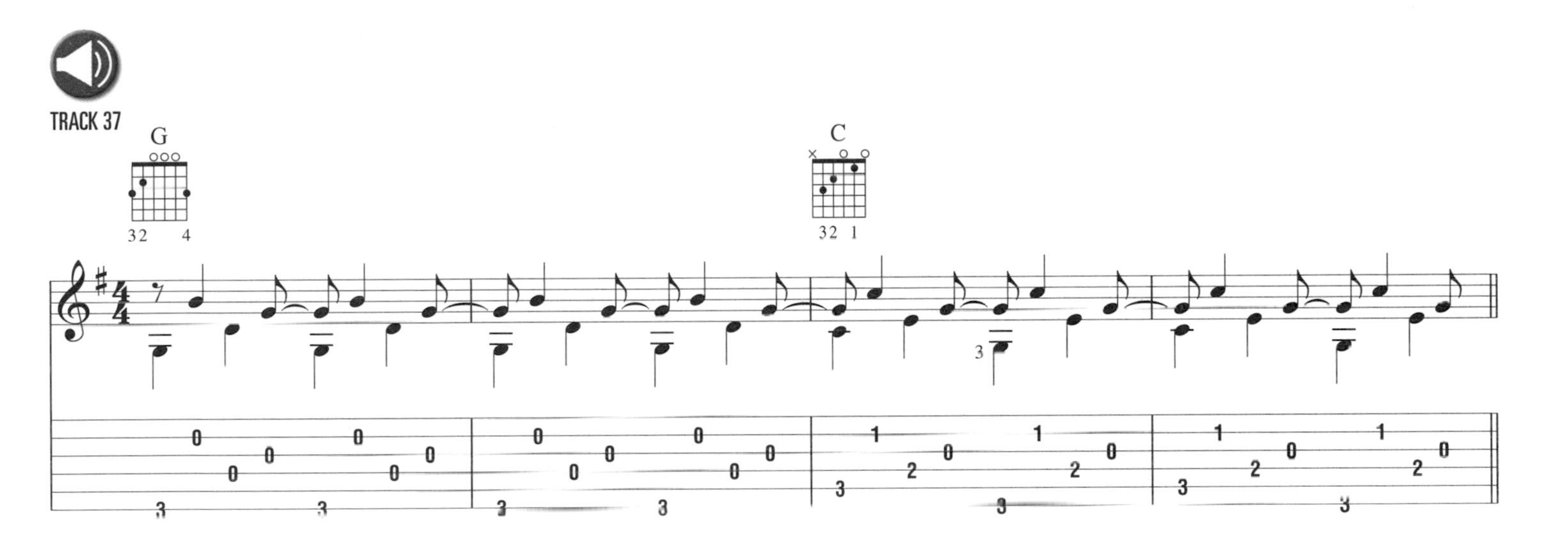

Now try this variation, which adds some motion to the bass between the G and C chords:

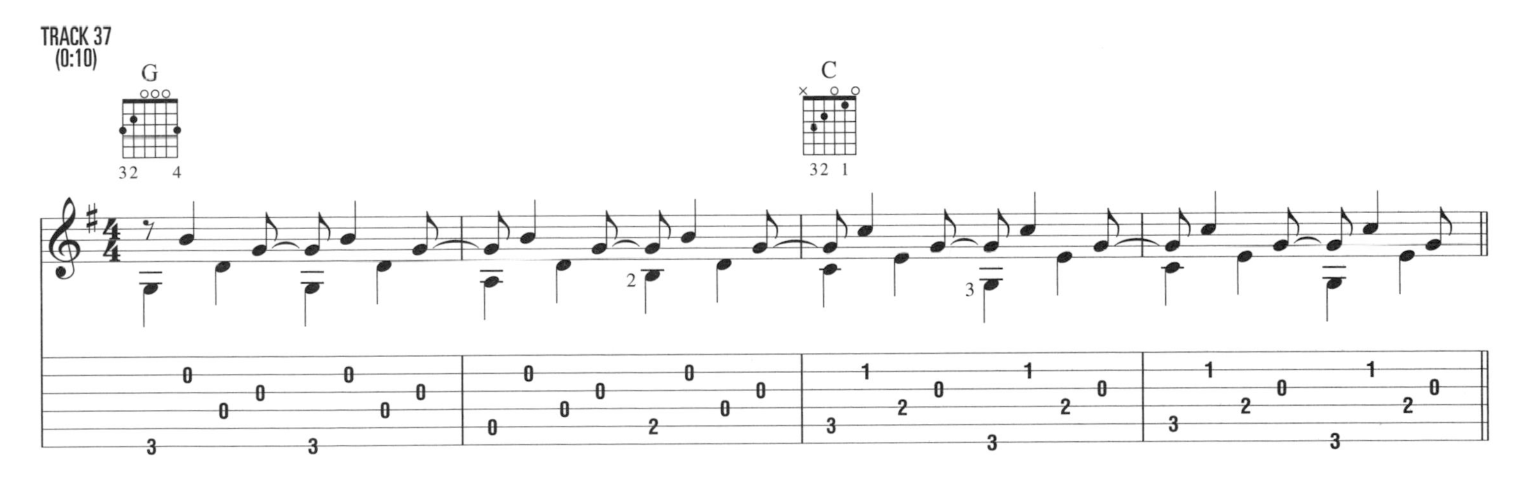

The second one adds a *moving bass line*. You'll notice that the lowest bass note moves slowly upward in the second measure, moving through A and B. This joins the G note in measure 1 to the C note in measure 3 by moving up one note at a time, from G through A and B to C. Any time you move the bass in a stepwise manner like this, from one chord to another, you're using moving bass lines. To play this moving bass line, keep your fingers fretting a G chord and simply pick your middle finger up from the fifth string to play that A bass note, then place it back on the 2nd fret for the B note before moving to the C chord.

Musical Steps

When you move your bass lines in a *stepwise* manner, the "steps" are either the distance of one or two frets. To know which notes to include in the steps, you can either use your ear to hear what sounds good, or you can use music theory to use notes from the scale affiliated with the key of the song you're playing. For a song in the key of G, use the G major scale. If you don't know enough theory to figure this out, you can use your ear (or find a book like *Music Theory for Guitarists,* from Hal Leonard).

One neat thing about moving bass lines is that you can easily extend or shorten them within your Travis-picking patterns. For instance, in our previous example, we alternated those moving bass lines with thumb notes on the fourth string. But if we eliminate those alternating bass notes just for the bass run, it doubles the speed of our bass line. This might feel a little funny at first, since your thumb plucks the *same* string twice in a row instead of keeping its plodding, string-jumping rhythm. But when you get comfortable with it, it's a great variation to have.

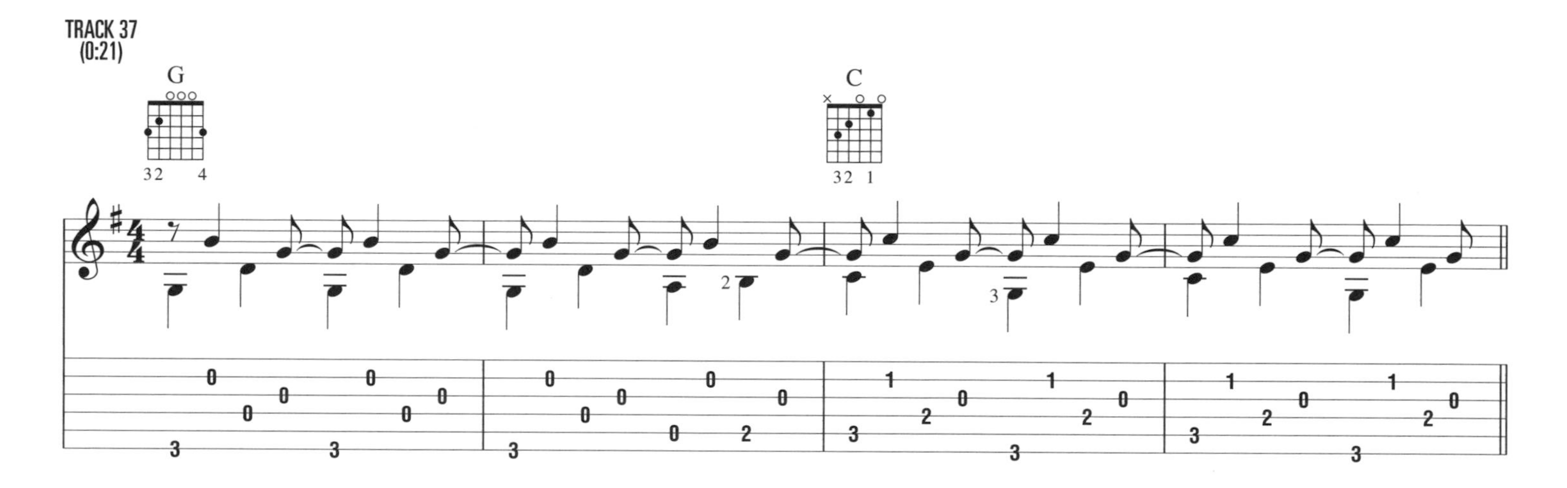

You can place moving bass lines between many sets of chords within a song. Let's try moving between G and Em:

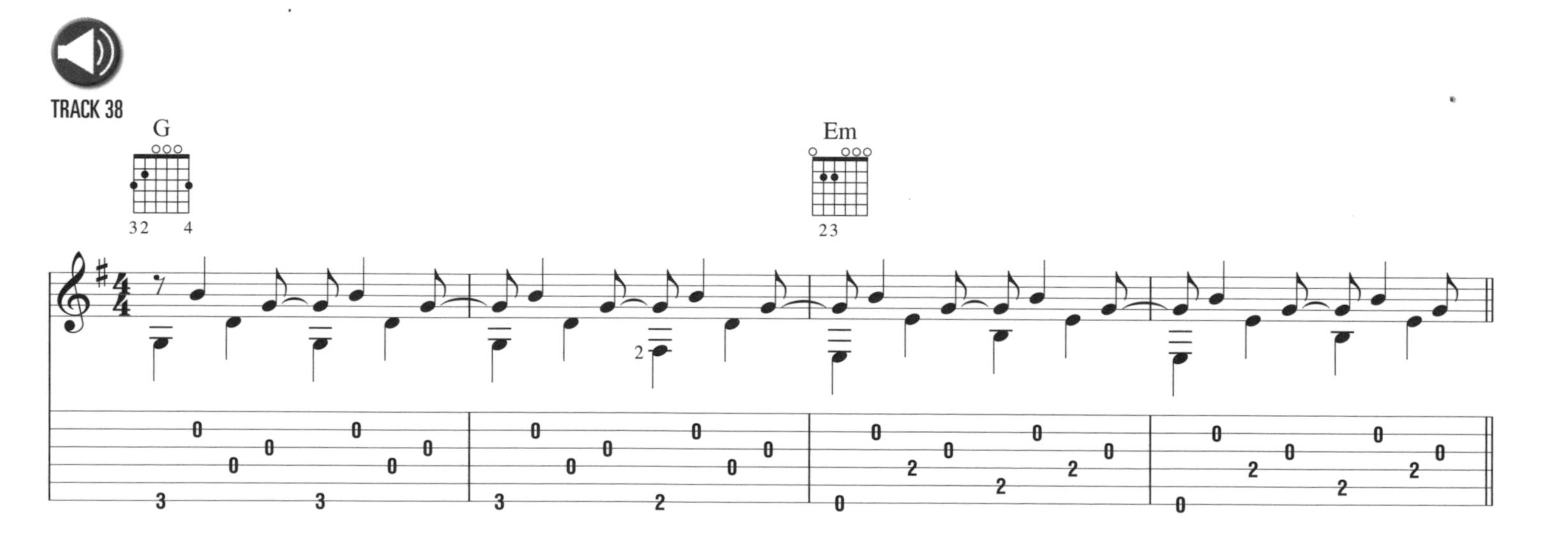

As you can see in the previous example, the bass moves from G—via F♯—to E of the Em chord. To play that F♯ note, you'll have to reach down with your middle finger. This means you won't be fretting the note on the fifth string—an essential part of the G chord—but this is OK as long as you don't play that string (which we won't!). In our previous G–C chord progression, we sped up our bass line. Now let's use this G–Em progression to see how we can stretch it out. One way you can do this is to move to the F♯ note earlier—at the beginning of measure 2—and hold that bass note for a full measure. Neither is *better*, but it allows you to see that there's more than one way to apply this technique, and you can use whichever approach sounds best to you in any given situation.

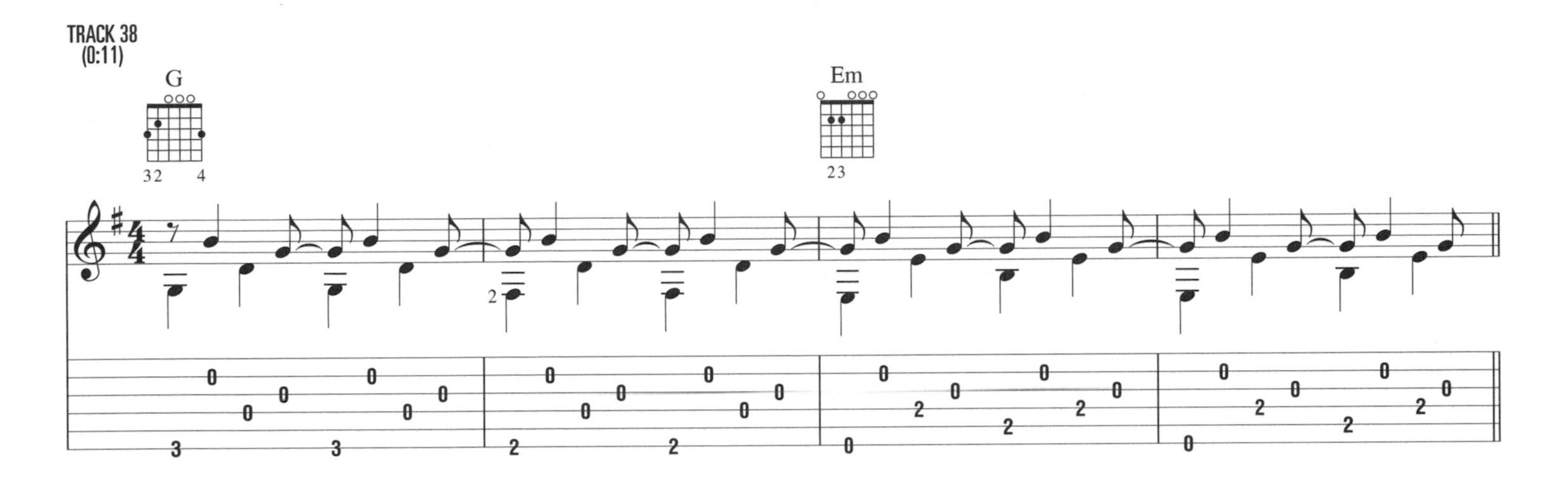

Let's look at another common moving bass line. This one moves from C to Am:

In chapter 2, we played a C pattern that sounded similar to Paul Simon's accompaniment for "The Boxer." Notice how, by adding this moving bass line, this pattern now sounds even *more* like the song. Check out how you need to move your middle finger down to the fifth string to fret the B note of the bass line. This means you're not holding down the note on the fourth string, which is part of the C chord. However, people still often play that open string, like we do here, and it sounds fine. In some circumstances, this is OK. Your ear will tell you when you need to avoid a string, so make sure to listen.

Again, we can stretch out this moving bass line if we want to, like this:

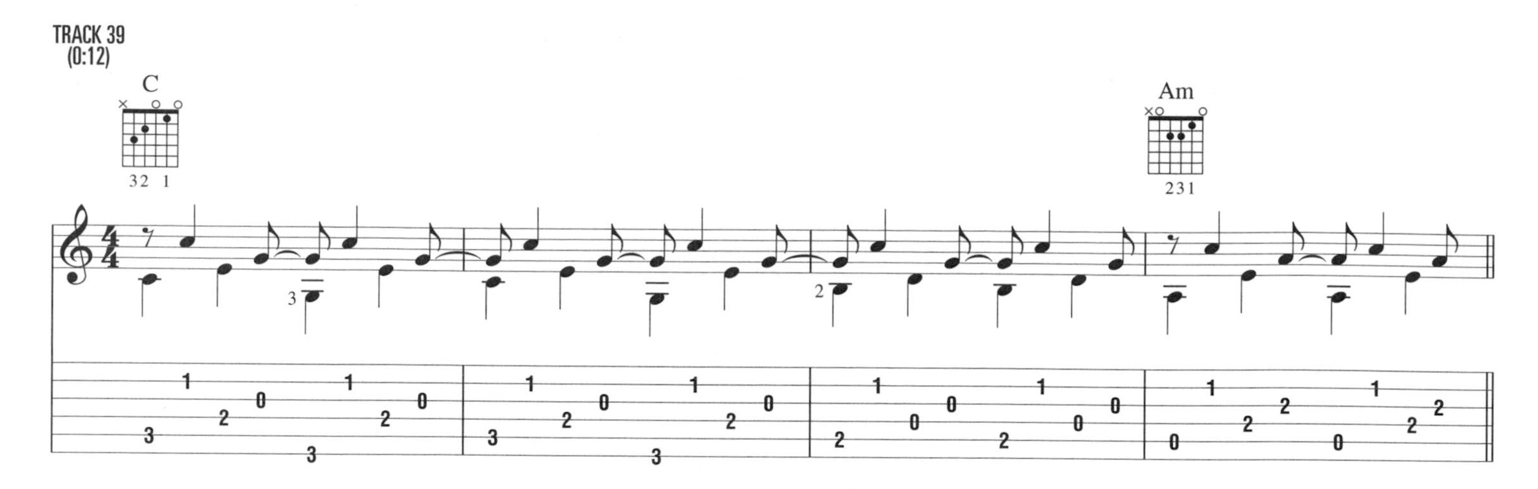

Now let's look at one that's a little more difficult. This time we'll move from E to A:

To fret the F# bass note, you'll have to reach down with your middle finger. This means you're not fretting the fifth string, but that's OK. We just won't play that string. The difficulty comes on the next note. Here, we have to reach up with our pinky to grab the G# note and—unless you have really long fingers—it's hard to keep your ring finger on the fourth string. So, we'll have to *simultaneously* move our middle finger up to the fourth string, which makes that reach with the pinky a bit easier.

Of course, this stretch and switch is still pretty tough to do quickly, so let's try another little trick: that open D string sounds fine with an E chord (and it's actually part of an E7 chord) so let's just leave it out as we move between chords. Now it's much easier and actually sounds better, too.

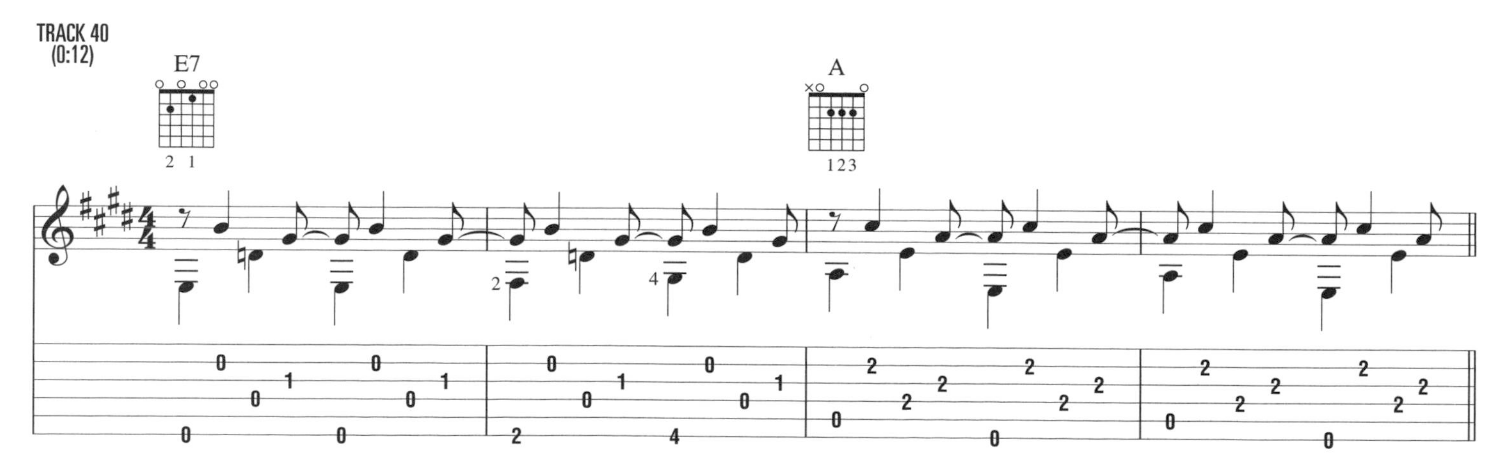

You can create countless other moving bass lines, as well. Any time you want to transition more smoothly between two chords, try applying these techniques to the chords you're playing and remember to use your ear.

PICKING VARIATIONS

At this point, you have all the tools to create a nearly limitless number of Travis-picking patterns to accompany your songs. All you need to do is make small adjustments to the patterns you already know. For instance, if you're playing the pattern with your middle and index fingers (leaving out the ring finger), simply play the index finger *first*, and you have a different-sounding pattern:

TRACK 41

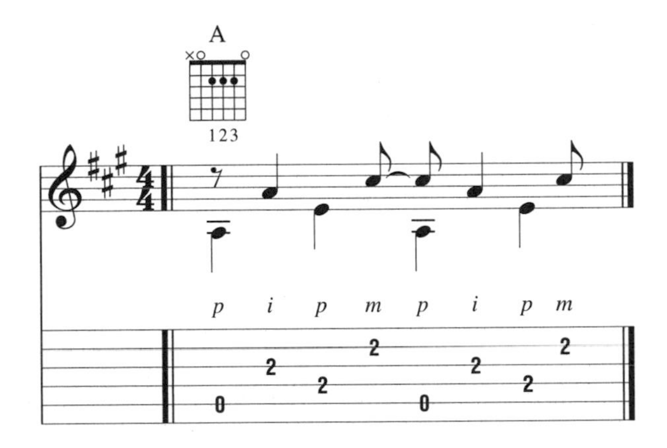

You can also try paring things back. This example leaves a note out of the pattern. Notice how it creates a brief pause in the pattern's flow:

TRACK 41
(0:07)

Or you could mix up all *three* fingers in many ways, like this one. It starts with the index, then uses the ring, middle, and ring fingers, in that order:

TRACK 41
(0:15)

Try playing each of the three fingers in sequential order to create a banjo roll–type accompaniment that takes three measures to cycle through, like this:

And don't forget those pinches. You could pinch more times within a measure or in different places, like this:

You could also pinch *two* notes with your fingers, instead of one, like this:

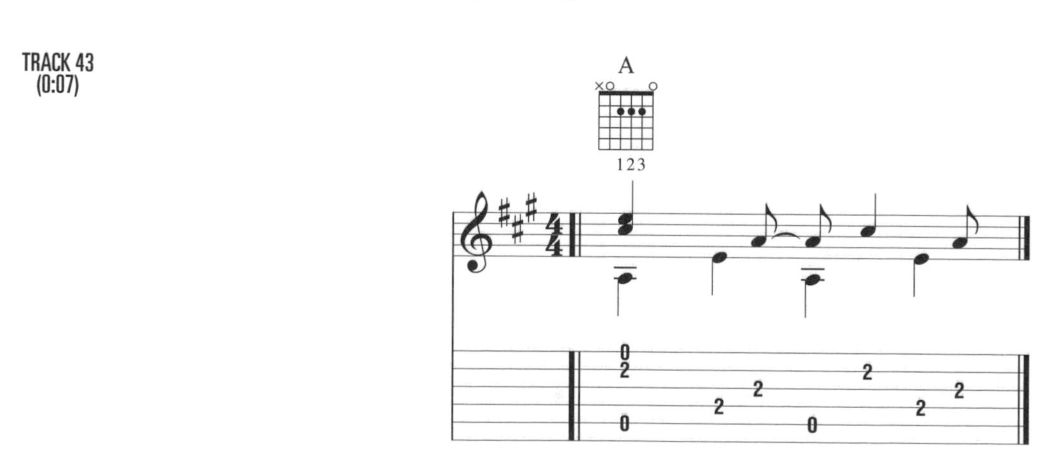

Bass lines can be modified, too. For instance, you could use just one finger to alternate with a quickly moving bass line, which puts a little more emphasis on the bass notes:

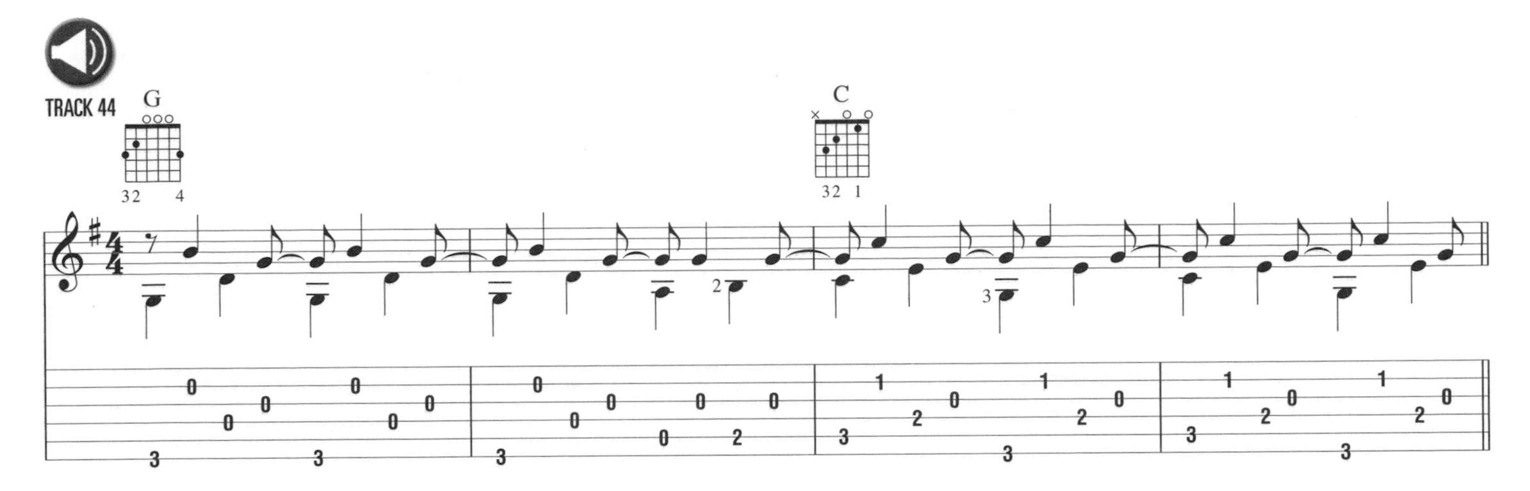

The point is, you can use your imagination to put all of these pieces together in limitless ways. Mix it up and come up with as many patterns as you like. Here are a few more to get you started. Notice how the second one leaves out a *bass* note:

SWEET SUNNY SOUTH

Let's try applying some of these ideas to the song we've been developing over the first two chapters, "Sweet Sunny South." You can see that I changed the pattern in the opening measures to include the ring finger. I thought this high G note added a little interest to the introductory measures. Then, as the vocal enters, I move back to the original pattern that we played behind the song. In measure 5, a walking bass line adds momentum to the D chord. Then, I play the pinch a little differently than the last chapter—this time on beat 2, instead of beat 1—to keep it out of the way of the vocals. Notice how I left out the pinch in the next measure; one pinch seemed to provide the best type of fill between vocal phrases. In the second half of measure 7, a walking bass line provides a little momentum to the G chord of the next measure.

Notice how I lift my fingers off the string on the last eighth note of measure 7. This gives my fingers time to fret the G chord, and since that note is part of the upcoming G chord, it also acts as an anticipation of the G chord. It's common to *anticipate* chord changes by jumping into the next chord just before the *downbeat* (beat 1) of a measure—another way to add a little forward momentum.

I also added more walking bass lines to several other places: between a G and C chord change (measure 9), from C back to G again (measure 11), and another D to G change (measure 16). But check out how I left *out* moving bass lines from the quick chord changes that happen in measures 12–15. Sometimes when chords are moving quickly, those changes are enough (moving bass lines can end up cluttering things too much). This is really a judgement call; however, feel free to try some out in these places, as well, to see if you like them. In the second-to-last measure, I resume the opening picking pattern for just one measure.

Sweet Sunny South

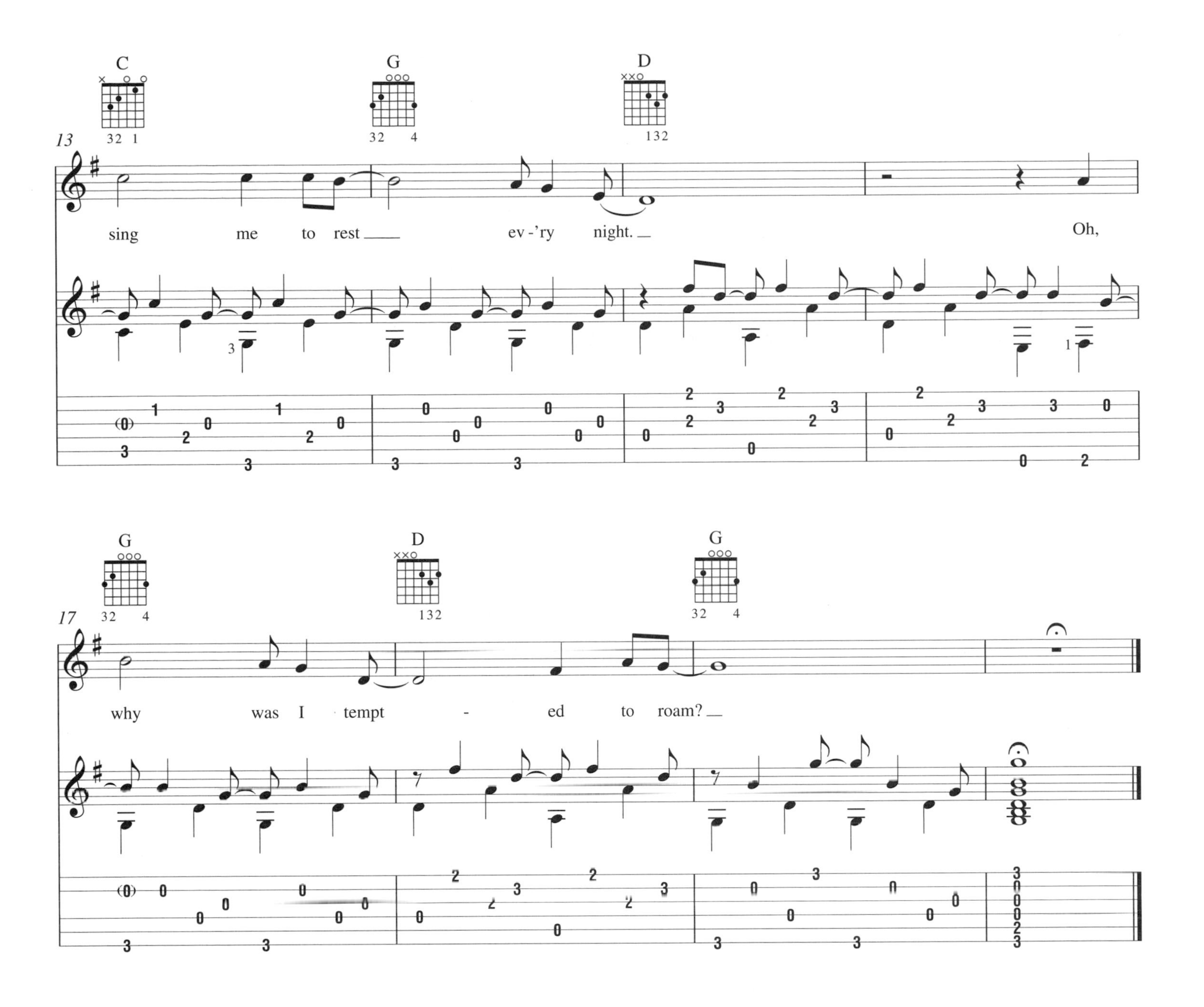

Now it's your turn to come up with as many Travis-picking variations as you can!

Variations Are Great, But...

Remember that, for these patterns, you're using your guitar to accompany songs. That means that you're trying to come up with the best *support* for the vocal at any given point. Sometimes that means adding in a cool variation here and there, but for the most part, the best accompaniments often repeat one pattern for long stretches. The point is that you have all of these tools to come up with great patterns. Once you have a pattern you like, it's often a good idea to keep that pattern going for at least a little while before changing it. Then, pinches and moving bass lines can be added in sparingly—again, to best support what's happening in the song at any given moment. At first, try not to include too many elements in one song. The more you accompany yourself, the more you'll get a feel for how much embellishment works in any given situation.

SECTION II
PLAYING MELODIES

While Travis-type picking is great for accompanying vocals, it's an equally good technique for fingerpicking solo guitar arrangements. In this section, we'll explore how you can weave together melodies and Travis-picking patterns. This type of picking works well for any melody in any genre, but it's especially popular with ragtime, blues, and folk pickers. When played in these other genres, it might not always be referred to as "Travis-picking." However, in whatever genre it's used, it follows the same underlying concept that we used in our Travis-picked accompaniment patterns, and it's a great way to build our technique and bridge the gap between popular Travis-style picking patterns and the Travis-picking played by the greats like Merle Travis and Chet Atkins.

CHAPTER 4:
ADDING MELODIES TO PICKING PATTERNS

Since you've finished the first section of this book, you already have the technical ability to create solo fingerpicking arrangements of songs. All you need to do is practice putting together melodies with your Travis-picking patterns, then work on spicing up the arrangements.

LEARN THE MELODY

When arranging any song, you need to first know the melody inside and out. This might sound ridiculous (of *course*, I know the melody!), but it's surprising how hard it can be to remember a melody *and* immediately play it on guitar. We're going to arrange the traditional song "Will the Circle Be Unbroken," so let's take a look at a simple version of the melody. When playing in this style, the melody is usually performed with the fingers. Play through the following example until you can play the melody without looking at the music.

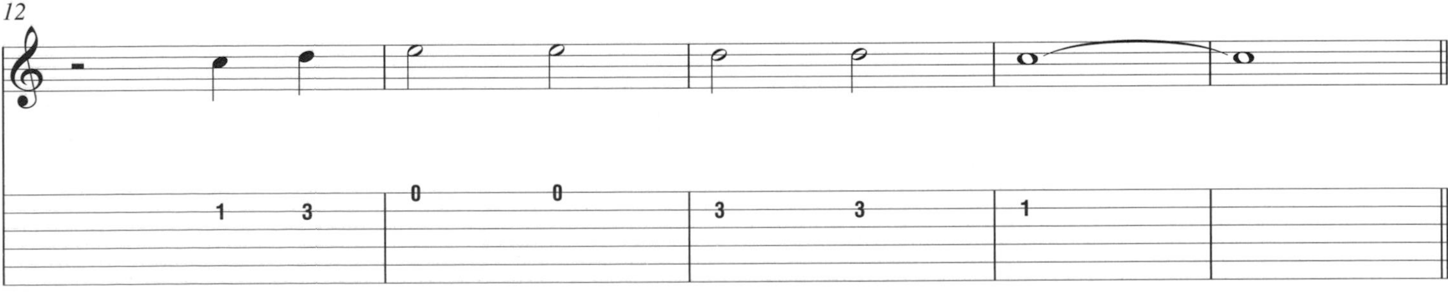

ADD BASS FROM THE UNDERLYING CHORDS

Once you're comfortable with the melody, it's time to add the bass notes. We'll play these only with the thumb, using our alternate-bass patterns. How do you know which notes to play? First, you'll need to either figure out the chords of the song by listening to it or by finding the chords from a reliable source. Then, a good way to start is by holding your hand in position to play each chord throughout its duration, moving any fingers you need to at any point to play melody notes. Here's our basic arrangement of the song's melody with bass. Keep your hand fretting the chord shapes shown above the music, but move individual fingers as shown in the notation to grab any notes that are found outside the chord shape.

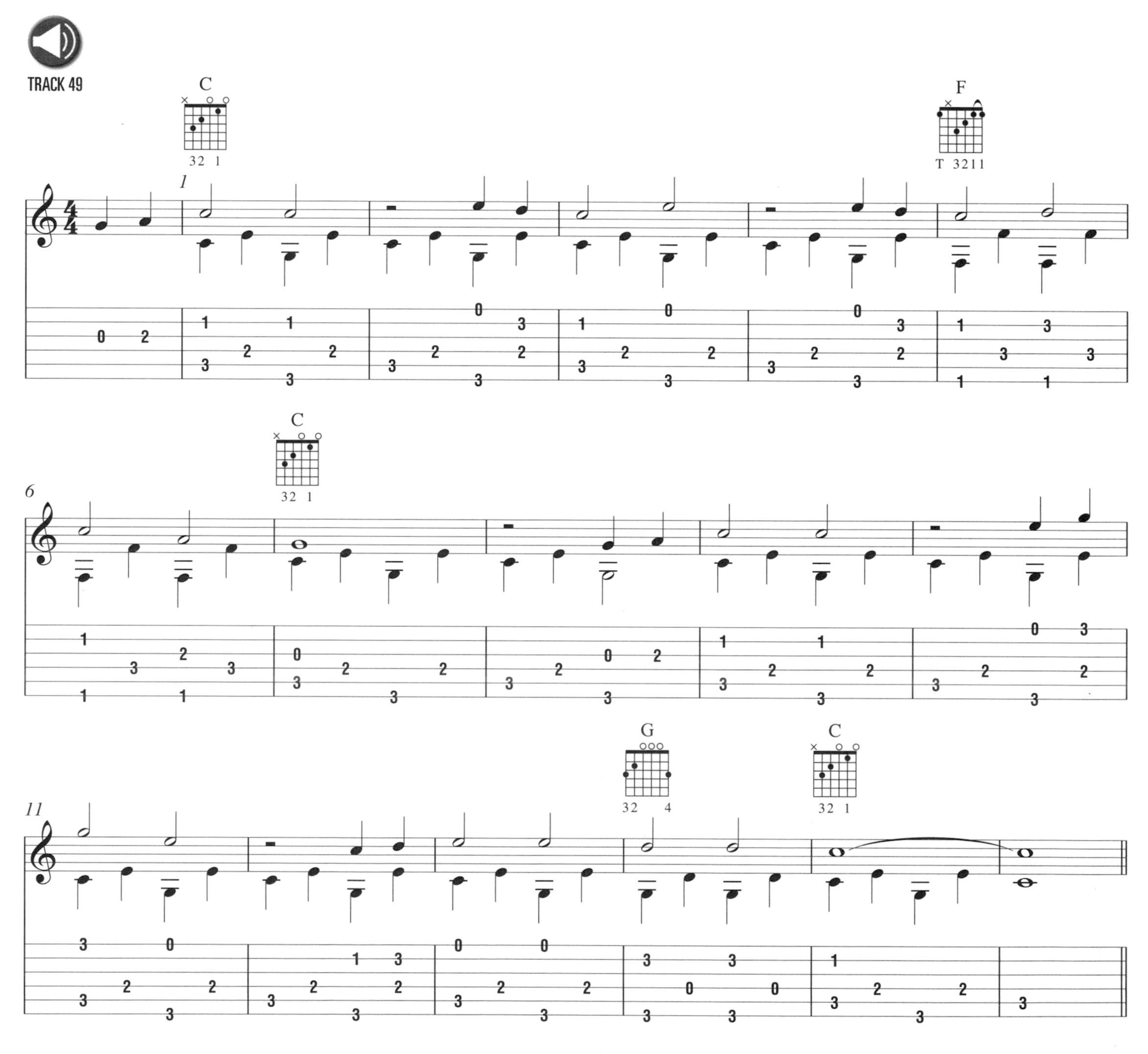

For the F chord, you'll need to fret the bass note with your thumb over the neck so you can play the D note on the 3rd fret of the second string that happens in the melody. *Thumb-fretting* like this is common when arranging a song this way, since you'll often need to access melody notes on the top strings. And if you play barre chords with a full barre, all of your fingers are used for the notes of the chord.

Once you can play through this example, you're already playing a song arrangement. But in the next chapters, we'll look at how you can play arrangements more easily and make them more interesting.

ADJUST FINGERINGS

When you played all the way through the last example, you might have noticed that the bass was briefly held at the end of measure 8. Why? The bass note that *would* be here (if we were continuing the pattern) is an E note on the 2nd fret of the fourth string, which is usually fretted by your middle finger, but it needs to move up a string for the melody note on beat 4. Meanwhile, your index finger is busy holding down the 1st fret of the second string while your ring finger is busy rocking between the 3rd fret of the fifth and sixth strings. Since we're not using our index finger for any melody notes in this measure, let's move it down to grab that E note, like this:

TRACK 50

We can make the same adjustment at the very beginning of the song, too. This will give us bass notes for the opening notes of the tune:

TRACK 51

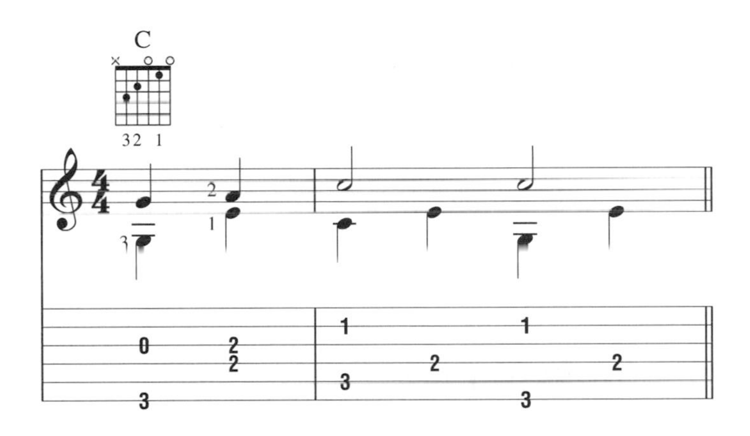

Aside from these places, there are no other areas where we need to make fingering adjustments. In other songs, you might need to switch your fingerings up much more often to grab all of the melody notes.

MELODIES AND BASS LINES *WITHOUT* CHORD SHAPES

The ultimate goal here is to play our bass patterns with melodies, and forming the chord shapes with your fingers is often a good way to start doing this, since it automatically gives you the bass notes for those chords. Of course, there will be times when you'll want to rock down to a bass note beneath a chord shape and you'll have to find the bass note that works (as we did in the first section of this book).

But, the ultimate goal doesn't rely solely on chord shapes. Once you're familiar with what bass notes work with each background chord, you only need those notes and the melody to play an arrangement. Sometimes you'll be fretting chord shapes and moving around those shapes, while at other times, you might be playing a bass line and melody notes that seem completely independent of chord shapes.

SYNCOPATE THE MELODY

This is the final step to really turn a song from a simple alternate-bass fingerpicking sound into a Travis picking–type sound. If you play through our previous arrangement, you'll see that the melody notes are *all* pinches. This won't be the case with all melodies, but to give a little forward momentum to our melodies, we'll *syncopate* parts of it so we will sometimes have notes falling between each beat. Let's start with the *pickup* (i.e., the first two notes of this example) and the first full measure. If we shorten the first melody note to an eighth note, the next melody note then falls between bass notes. So, in the first full measure, let's play the first melody note with a pinch, but the next melody note an eighth note early. Compare this to what we played in our first arrangement of "Will the Circle Be Unbroken" (pg. 40) and you'll see that it gives a feeling of forward momentum.

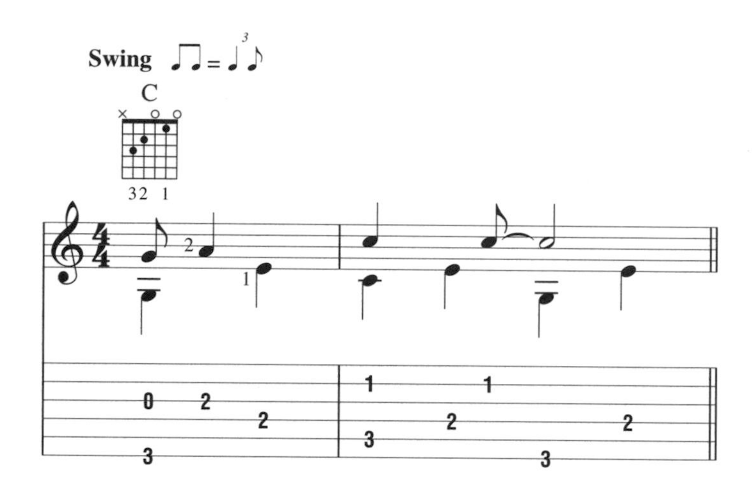

In the previous example, you might have noticed that playing those first two notes on the same string can be difficult. You can play this several ways: if you're adept at *double-picking*, use your index finger for both of these notes; if you find this too difficult to master, try bringing your middle finger down to pick the second note in the sequence (the A note). Either way will work, and different players will play the line differently. Try both ways and use the method that feels most comfortable for you.

WILL THE CIRCLE BE UNBROKEN

Let's look at the full song again, now adding syncopation to a few melody notes in a similar way. Note, however, that syncopation isn't used on *every* note (if it were, then every single melody note would fall between bass notes). While you *can* play it completely syncopated (and it sounds fine), mixing in a moderate amount of syncopation usually varies things a little better and makes it sound more interesting than a completely syncopated melody line.

Here's our completed arrangement of "Will the Circle Be Unbroken." Notice that the first measure only shows two beats. Whenever you have a short measure that leads into the first measure of a song, it's called a *pickup* measure.

TRACK 53

Will the Circle Be Unbroken

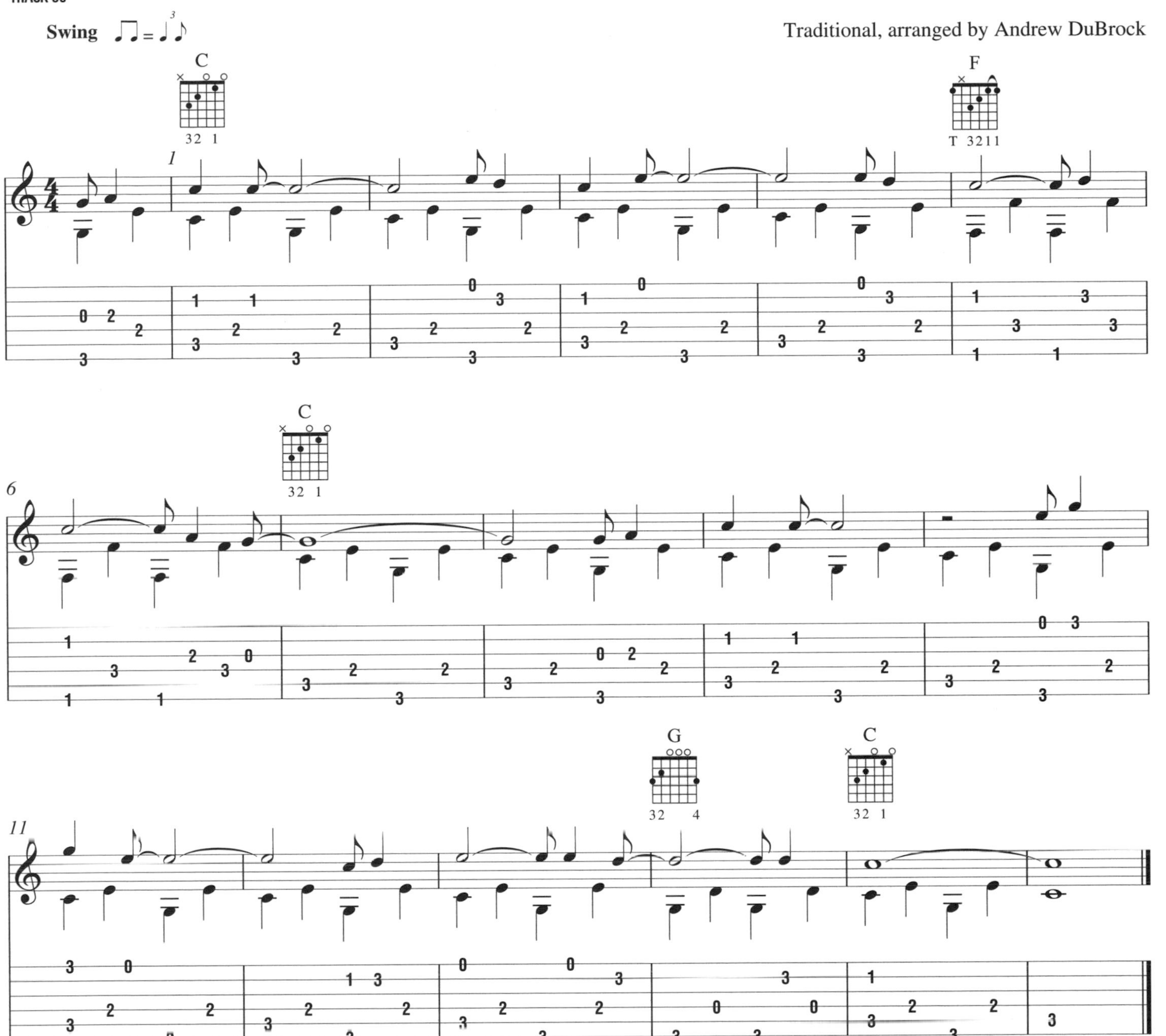

You can arrange most any melody this way and vary things quite a bit, depending on how you syncopate that melody. In the next chapter, we'll look at a few ways to enhance and fill out arrangements like this.

Palm Muting

A nice touch to solo arrangements like this is to add a little *palm muting* to the bass notes. To palm mute, lightly lay your pick-hand palm against the bass strings as you play. Try using the fleshy, outside edge of your hand—the bottom part of your hand, farthest from your thumb—so that your thumb has freedom to move. If you hear the notes muted completely, loosen up the pressure a little. This technique adds a nice thumping sound to the bass notes and also dulls their volume, allowing the melody notes to cut through even more.

CHAPTER 5:
ENHANCING MELODIES

Playing full songs by combining melody and a bass line sounds great on its own, but there are a few more things we can do to dress up these arrangements. In this chapter, we'll look at a few ways to enhance Travis-picking arrangements and apply these techniques to our version of "Will the Circle Be Unbroken" from chapter 4.

FILL OUT THE ARRANGEMENT

In the last chapter, we saw how syncopating our melody can add more of a driving feel to our arrangements. But we can instill this driving feel even further by adding notes on the offbeats that aren't part of the melody. For instance, here's our pickup and opening measure:

TRACK 54

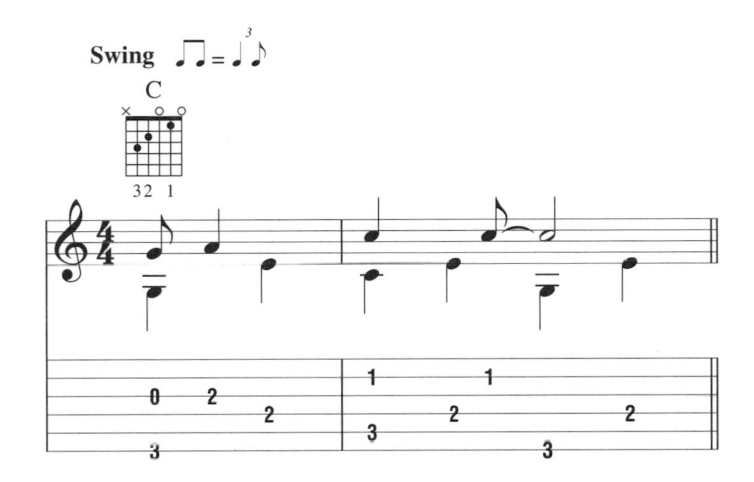

Now let's add a few offbeat notes on the open G string, like this:

TRACK 54
(0:07)

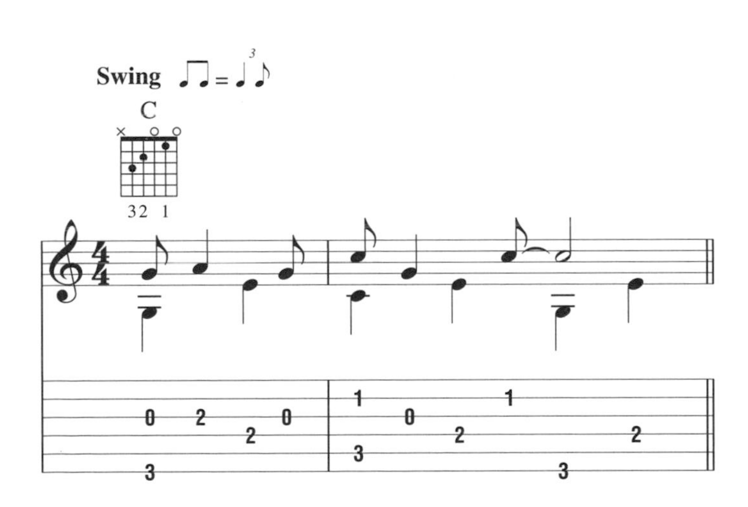

This is a simple and effective way to fill things out. But beware: if you fill out an arrangement like this and play everything at the same volume, it will sound like an endless blast of eighth notes. When you use this technique, make sure to highlight the melody notes by playing them a little louder (and by backing off on the filler notes).

So, we can fill out our arrangement by adding non-melody notes on the offbeat. Aside from just picking these notes, we can also use *hammer-ons* or *pull-offs* to fill things out and even make some passages easier to play. Let's take another look at the previous example. The melody in this example starts with two notes on the same string—something that can be a bit difficult to play—but by adding a hammer-on from the first note to the second, this becomes much easier to pick since you don't have to quickly play two notes in a row.

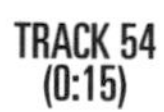

Let's try this concept over a measure of the F chord. Here's what we played in the last chapter:

After we play the first melody note, let's add a filler note on the offbeat. We can then add a hammer-on to the 2nd fret to fill things out even more. Then, since we have several filler notes in a row, let's play the melody note again on the "&" of beat 2, which helps us hear the melody over all of these other parts.

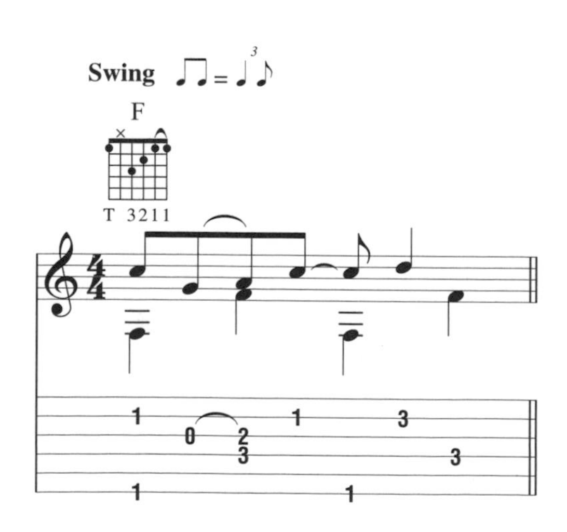

EMBELLISH THE MELODY

Adding filler notes is one way to thicken an arrangement, and another way is to *embellish the melody*. Let's start with the last phrase of "Will the Circle Be Unbroken":

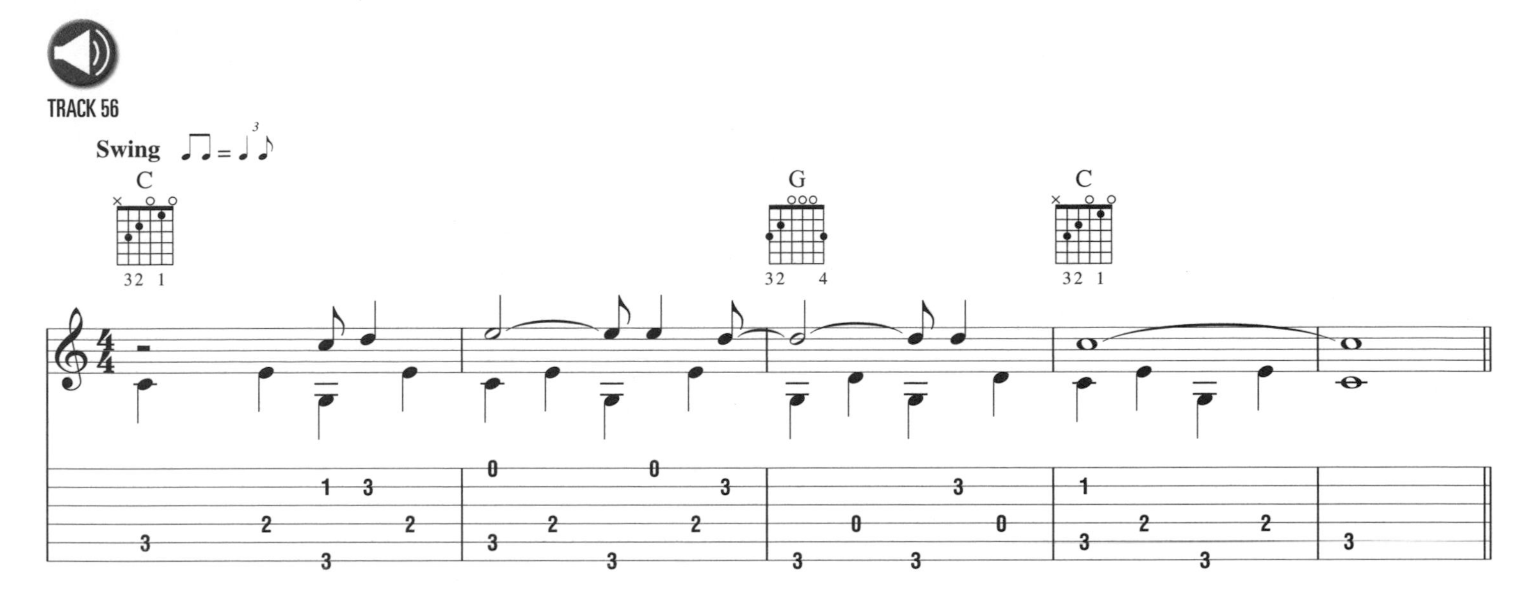

I'm first going to embellish the E note in the second measure by adding a high G to the melody just before it, and then a pull-off to the E, which brings out this melody a little more.

We don't need hammer-ons or pull-offs to embellish notes. Let's try embellishing the melody in the next measure by adding an E on beat 3, just before the D melody note an eighth note later—a similar embellishment to the previous measure.

We'll put it together by adding a few filler notes. Also, let's jump to the last melody note, C, an eighth note earlier for a smoother line, like this:

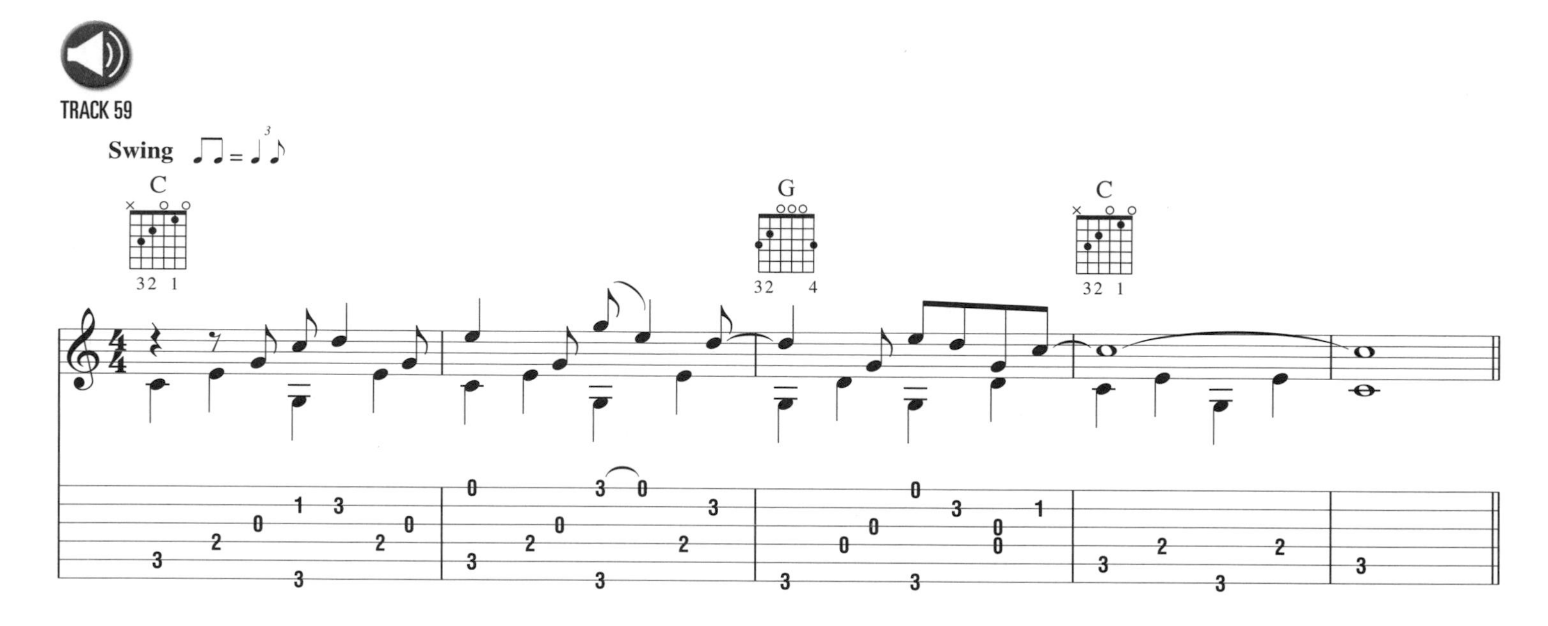

Bends also give us a unique way to embellish the melody. Here's our two-measure sequence over the F chord:

Now check out how this bend adds a bluesy quality to our melody (one of the reasons it's popular in fingerpicking blues circles).

SLIDES WORK, TOO

In "Will the Circle Be Unbroken," we've used hammer-ons, pull-offs, and bends to embellish our melody line. But don't forget about *slides*, which will work well, too.

DOUBLE STOPS ACCENT MELODY NOTES

Another tool you can use to highlight melody notes is to add a harmony note (*double stop*) to them. Let's try this over the following section of "Will the Circle Be Unbroken":

TRACK 62

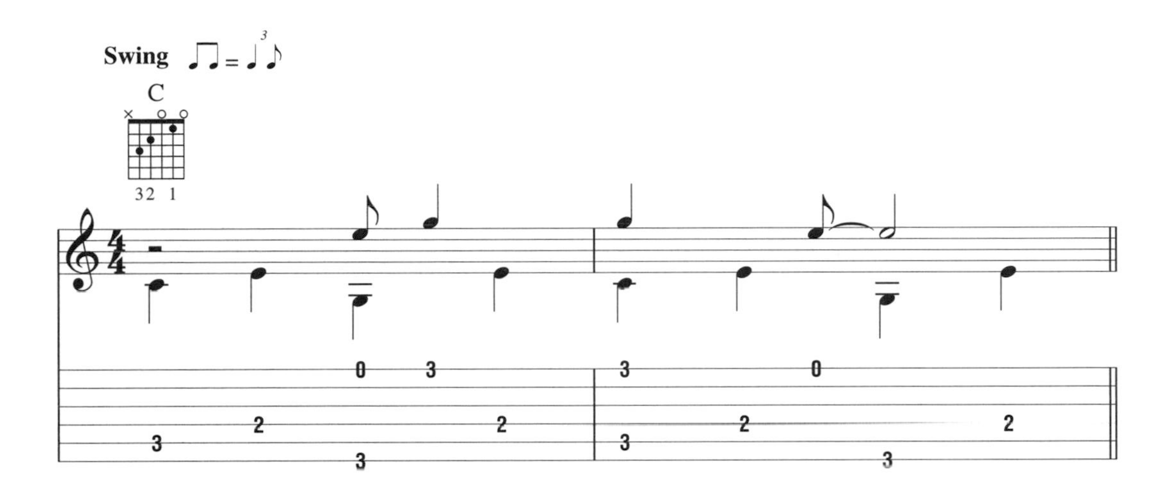

We'll harmonize the melody notes in the second measure by using the C root as our harmony note because it sounds good (and it's easy to grab!). We'll also add a few notes on the open G string to fill out the rhythm.

TRACK 63

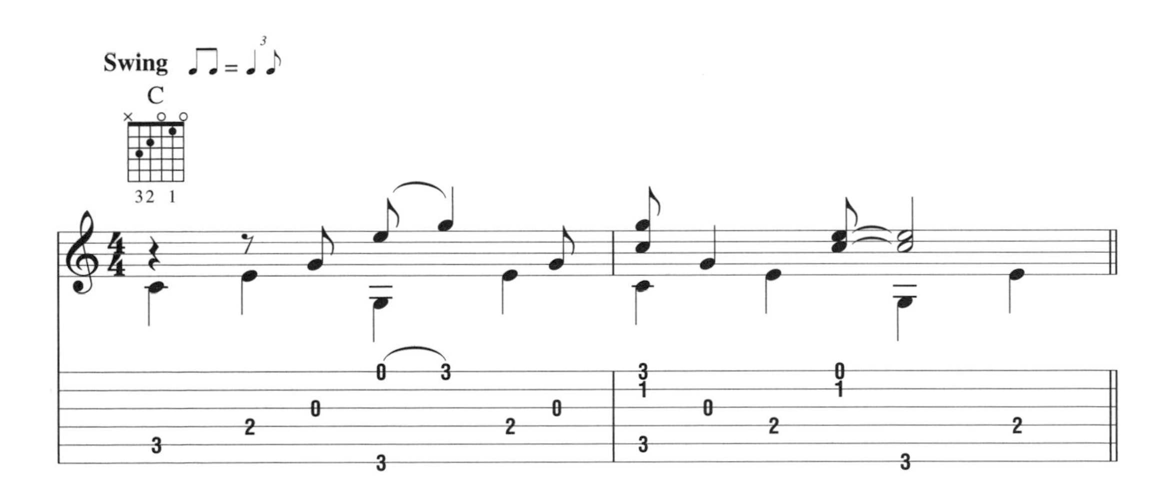

EMBELLISH THE CHORDS AND BASS LINE

When you play with others, it's important to play the same chord progression (there's nothing worse than hearing clashing chords played together!), but when you're playing a solo guitar arrangement of a song, you're much freer to *embellish the chords and bass line*. While you don't want to deviate too far, you can certainly use a different chord here and there or add an extra chord change or two. In "Will the Circle Be Unbroken," I like to add a quick G chord at the end of phrases to highlight the change back to C. Here's how the phrase looks before we add in the G:

Here it is with the quick G chord. It's a subtle change and there's really only one note that defines the change to G—instead of an E note on the fourth string, we're playing a D—but this change provides a little extra momentum back to the beginning of our next phrase over the C chord.

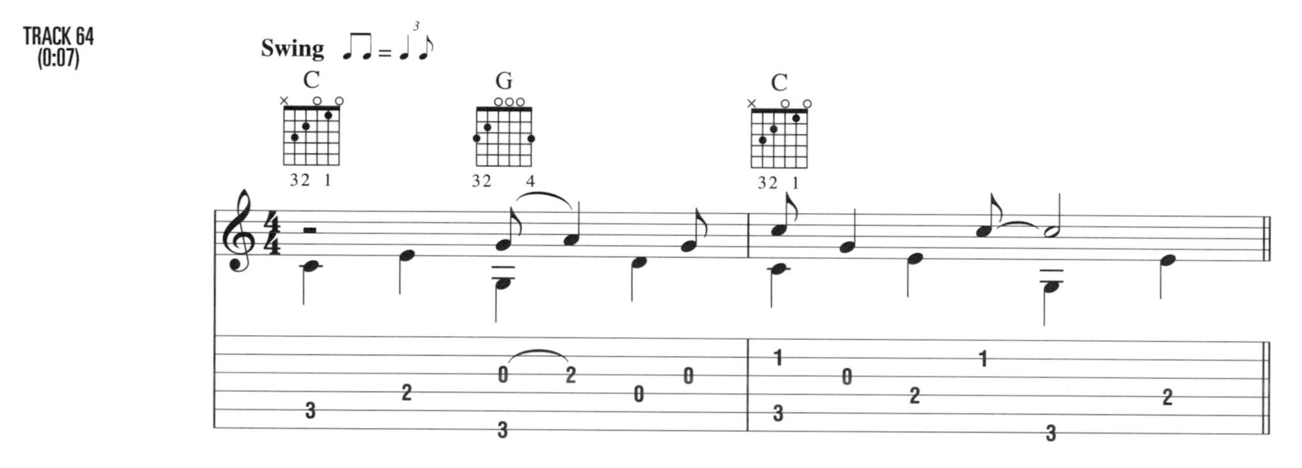

It's also common in the context of our C–F chord change to move through C7, which accentuates the shift to F. Here's that passage without the C7:

Now let's create a C7 chord by adding in the harmony B♭ note under the E melody note in the third measure.

TRACK 66

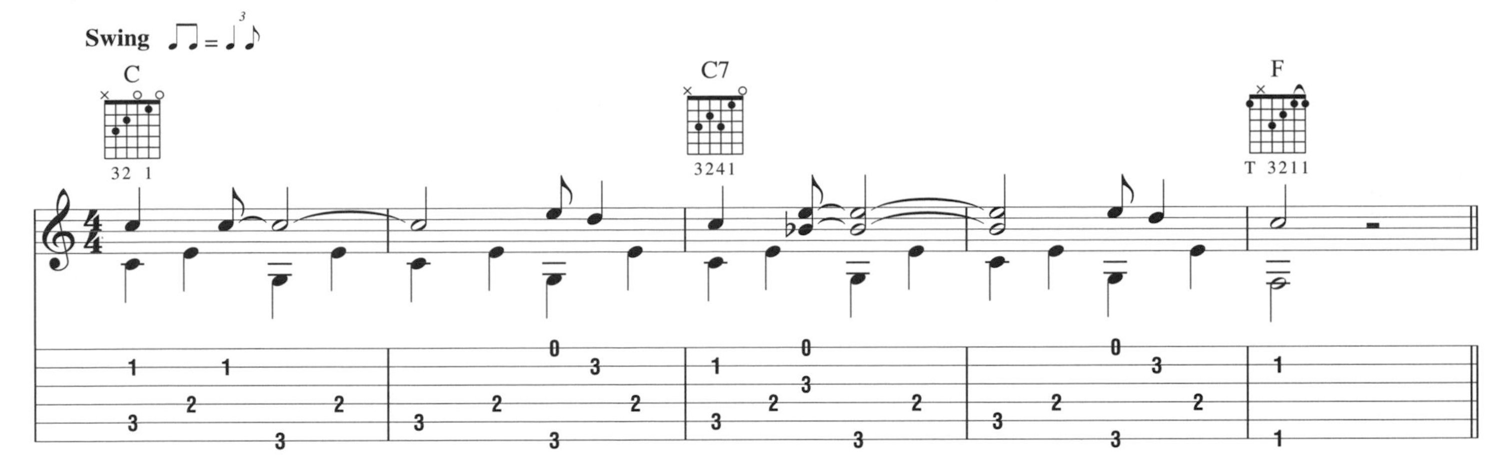

We added walking bass lines to our accompaniment picking patterns in the first section of this book, and we can do the same thing when we play solo arrangements. Let's spruce up this C–F chord change further by adding a walking bass line in the fourth measure. Notice how we walk through B♭ to again highlight a C7 sound (B natural is part of a Cmaj7 chord, while B♭ is part of a C7—or dominant—sound).

TRACK 67

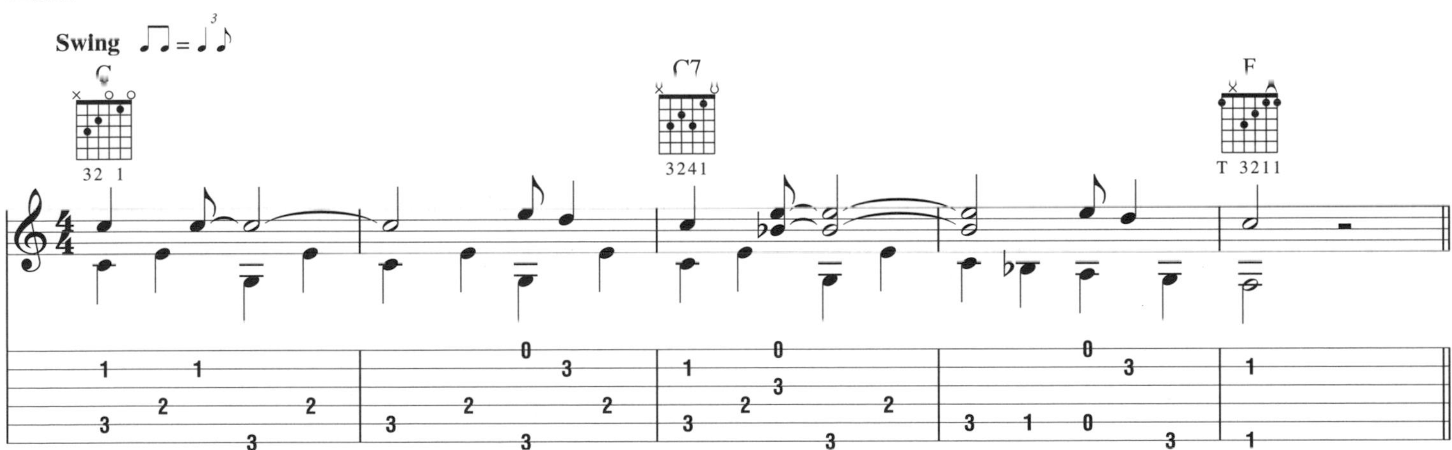

WILL THE CIRCLE BE UNBROKEN

Now let's see how all of these things look within a complete arrangement of "Will the Circle Be Unbroken." Throughout this version of the song, filler notes have been added on occasional offbeats to keep the rhythm moving forward. Notice how this arrangement starts on a G chord—duplicating the quick G "turnaround" move we used in the middle of the song. Another quick G happens in the penultimate measure of the tune. Here, notice how I've added filler notes in the melody. This is often found in acoustic blues tunes like the Piedmont picking of Etta Baker.

Will the Circle Be Unbroken

Traditional, arranged by Andrew DuBrock

SECTION III
ADVANCED TRAVIS PICKING

In this final section, we'll look at more-advanced Travis-picking techniques all over the neck of your guitar—not just down at the nut. We'll look at specific techniques that the Travis-picking masters used to play their great licks and patterns. In chapter 6, we'll go directly to the source—Merle Travis himself—and study his unique style of picking. Then, in chapter 7, we'll look at one of the most influential proponents of Travis-style picking: Chet Atkins.

CHAPTER 6:
PICKING LIKE MERLE

While many people Travis-pick and even emulate Merle Travis's style, few actually play like Merle did. That's mainly because Merle Travis used only two fingers to pick his dense arrangements—his thumb playing the thumping rhythm while *only his index finger* plucked out melodies on top. Most fingerpickers that followed also used their middle finger, too (and some use their ring and even pinky fingers!).

Travis achieved his thumping bass by plucking vigorously enough with his thumb that he often hit multiple strings in one picking motion. He frequently referred to his style of playing as "thumbstyle." Here's how that sounds over a barred G chord:

TRACK 69

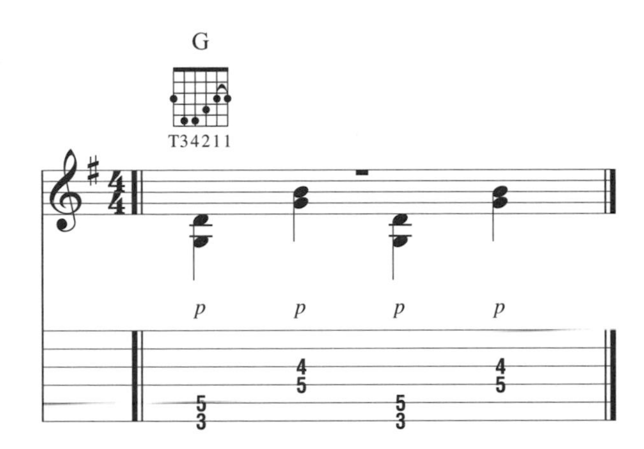

Don't worry too much about precision here. Sometimes you'll hit one string, but sometimes you'll hit several strings. Travis even plucked all the way through to the first string on occasion. If you aim for a group of strings, after a while you'll generally hit the same strings fairly consistently.

EXTENDED CHORD SHAPES AND FINGERINGS

Along with his thumping bass, Travis played more complex chord forms than we've explored yet in this book—*extended chord shapes* like these 7th and 9th chords. Here's how they're most commonly fingered:

TRACK 70

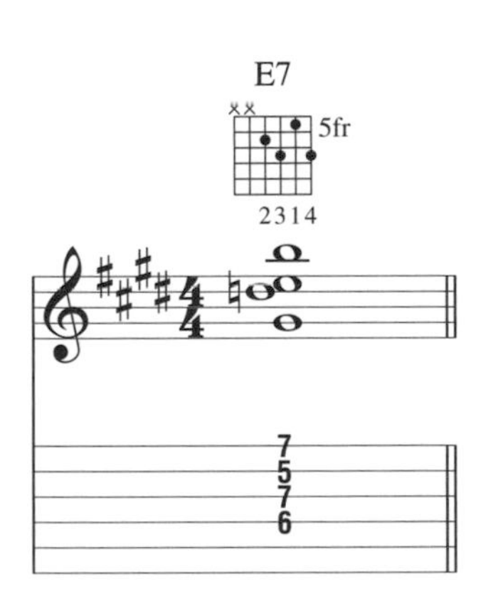

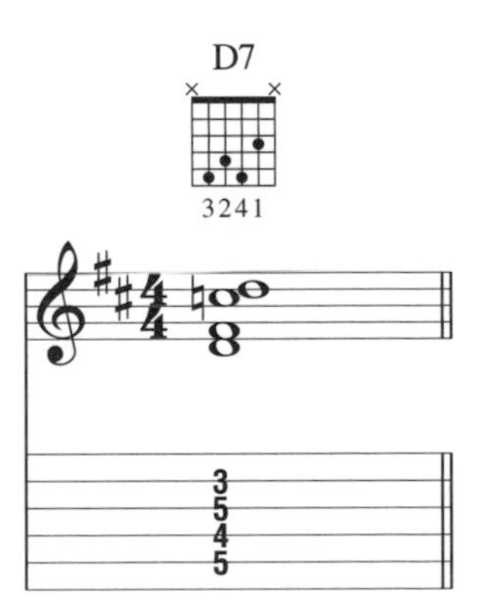

Travis often used his thumb to fret *two* strings over the neck of his guitar. So, instead of the more-common D9 and E7 fingerings (pg. 55), he'd add that double-fretted thumb beneath the chord voicings to get patterns like these:

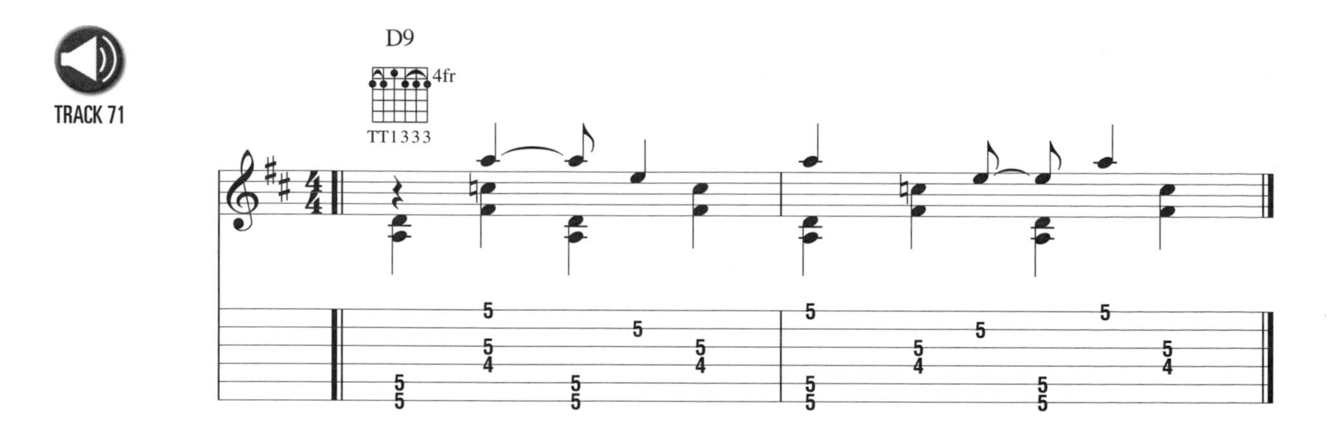

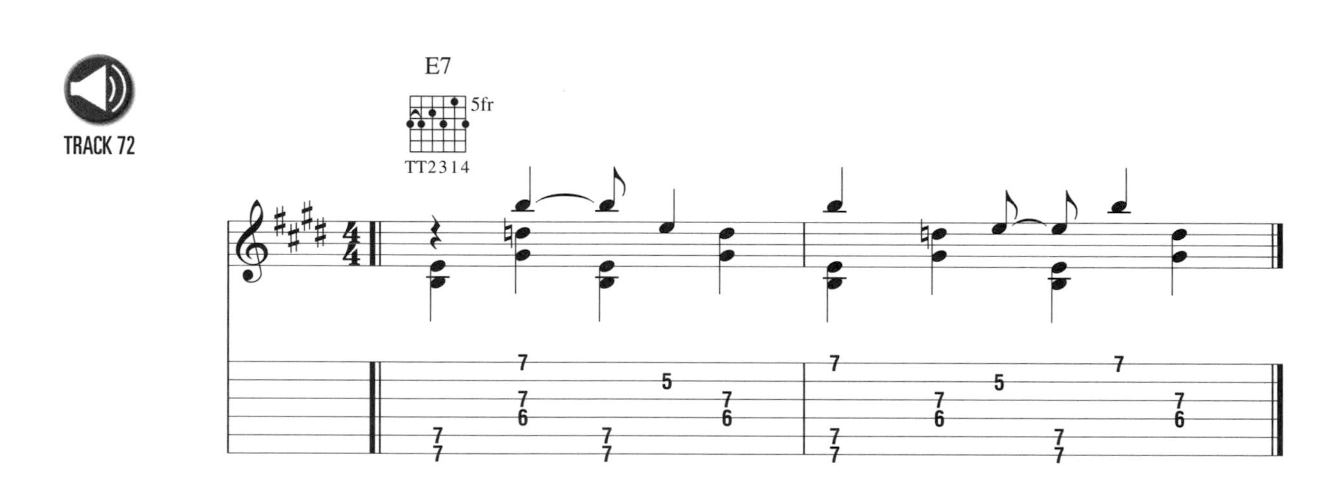

For the D7 shape, Travis fretted two strings with his *ring* finger, allowing him to play patterns like this:

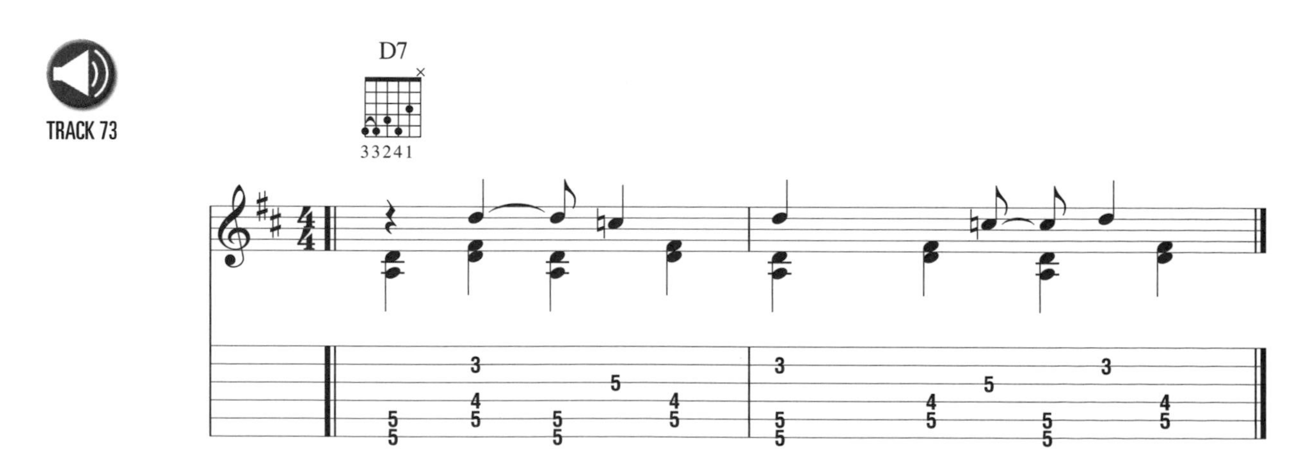

Fretting two strings with any finger (or thumb) is quite difficult—especially if you have smaller fingers. If you have trouble playing any of these patterns, adapt them to your fingers by playing only one string for the lower bass grouping, like this for the D7 chord:

Or, you could simply play the pattern over the standard chord:

As an alternative, you can rock between bass notes. For the D7 chord, you'd do that with your ring finger, like this:

Travis himself, however, didn't usually play three-string bass patterns like the previous example; instead, he most often alternated between two bass notes. But for some chords, Travis would remove his thumb to alternate with a lower open string, like this for our E7 shape:

Travis would also do this for a barred A chord, like this:

You can try this out on other chords, but note that it won't work for too many chords. The lower open string needs to be a note in the chord to really work.

ROLL PATTERNS

Another staple of Travis's style is the use of rolls for quick fills or complete passages. *Roll patterns* often play three strings in sequential order, repeating them over-and-over to create a "rolling" feel. To see how this works, let's look at one pattern and shape that Travis might use over a C9 chord.

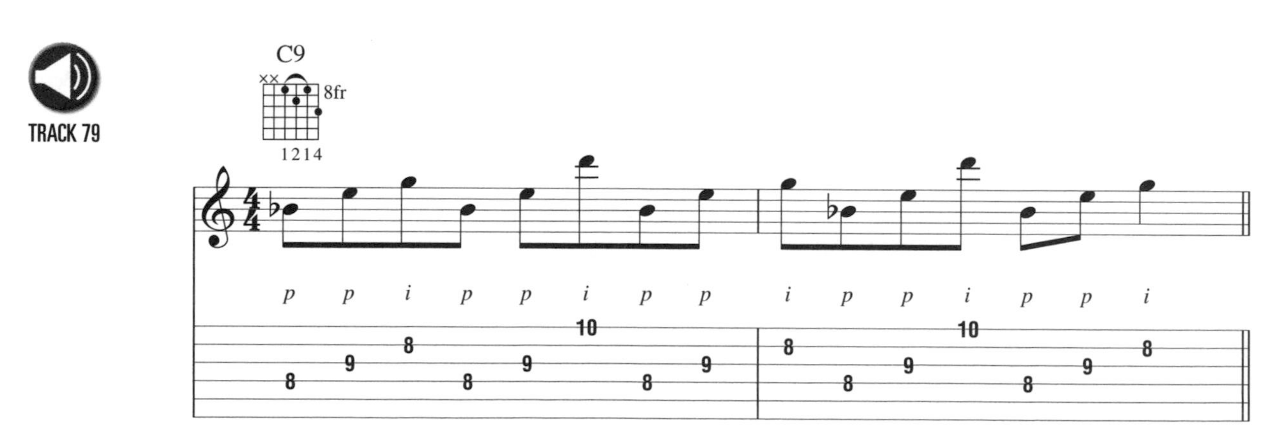

Pay careful attention to the fingering in the previous example. Since Travis only used his thumb and index finger, he'd have to play the first two notes of every three-note group with his thumb. Of course, if you're using your index and middle fingers, you can shift your index finger down to play every other thumb stroke and use your middle finger instead of the index finger here.

Travis often used these rolls in conjunction with open strings—particularly the high E string. Here's a shape he liked to use for E7:

Here are several shapes he used for a G6 sound:

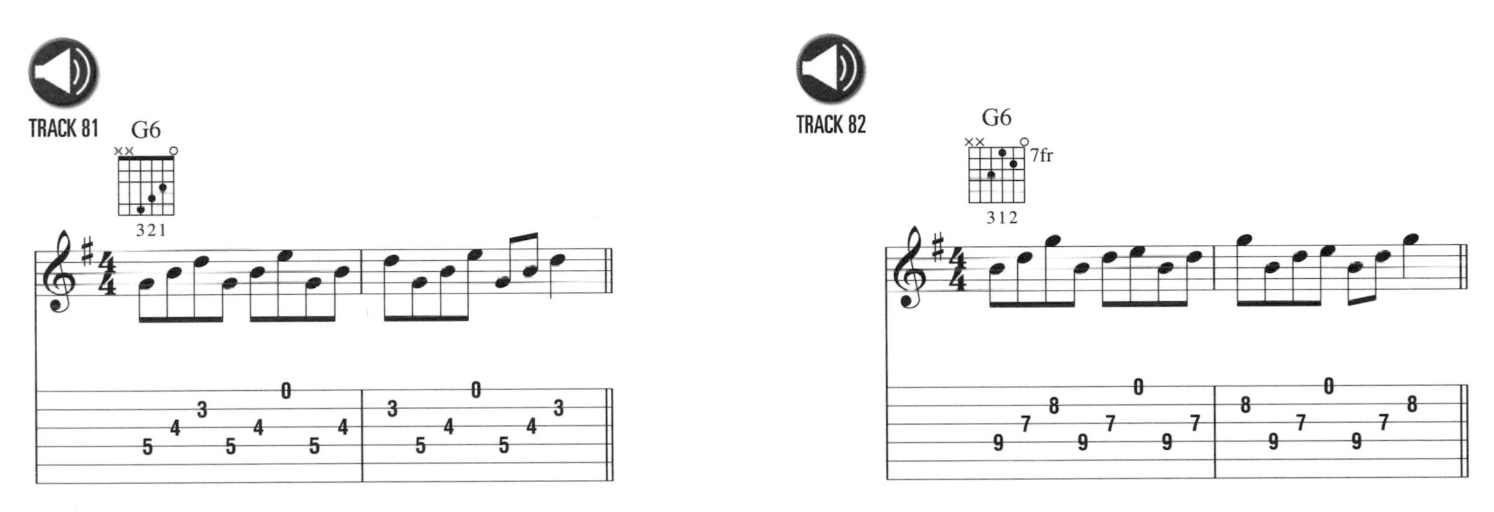

Note how all of these examples use the same picking pattern on the top four strings. Travis was fond of this pattern and used it most often. It works with many other chord shapes, too. Try it with this shape for a D9 sound:

Plus, you can slide many of these shapes around for different chords. Here's the E7 shape slid down two frets for another D9 variation:

RAG-TAG

Now let's try these techniques in a song similar to what Travis played. "Rag-Tag" utilizes a popular ragtime chord progression and follows an AABBA format. In the A section, note how the bass line at the end of the second measure includes a G♯ note that walks up to A. Travis often played bass lines like this—of course, using his thumb over the neck to play it (which is quite a stretch!). The B section is completely built on rolls, using chord shapes that work over the same chord progression.

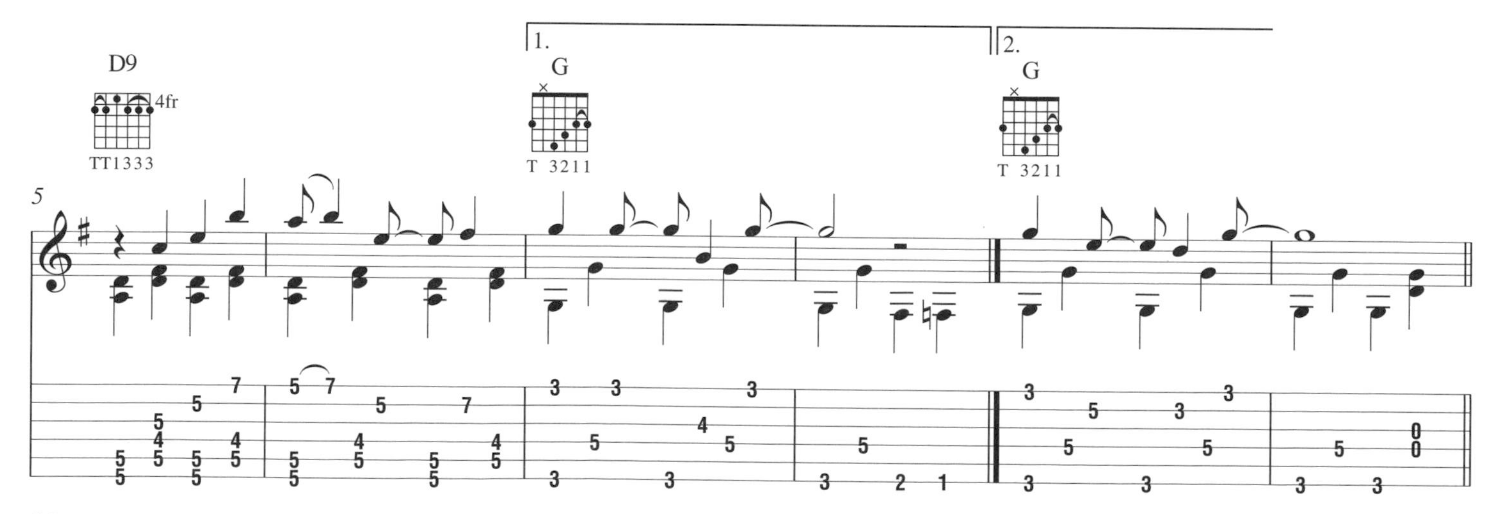

B
E9
6fr
123
A13
5fr
123
11
D9
5fr
13
G6
7fr
312
15
A
E7
5fr
TT2314
A7
5fr
T 1211
19
D9
4fr
TT1333
G
T 3211
23

CHAPTER 7:
PICKING LIKE CHET

Merle Travis gave "Travis-picking" its name, but another guitarist brought the technique to the masses. Few guitarists have made as big of a mark on music as Chet Atkins. Atkins integrated Travis's style into his own developing sound, then went on to become a household name. As a prominent Nashville producer, artist, and session musician, Atkins popularized Travis-picking in ways that Travis himself never could.

PRECISION PLAYING

Atkins' playing was more precise than Travis's. Instead of hitting groups of bass notes with his thumb, Atkins would deliberately pick out bass lines, focusing on single notes or specific groups of notes (often not more than two). Travis used just his thumb and index finger, but Atkins added his middle finger (and sometimes his ring finger) into his picking patterns.

Atkins was also very precise in his ability to separate the bass and melody. His palm muting was impeccable, and his melody and bass lines always sounded like two guitars playing independently.

ROLL PATTERNS, OPEN STRINGS, AND RUNS

Travis used roll patterns in his playing, and so did Atkins. The same pattern Travis used was also one of Atkins' favorites.

Atkins used more roll patterns, like this one:

Either of these two roll patterns can be adapted to many different chord shapes and open strings. For instance, here's an F♯7 shape using the previous roll pattern:

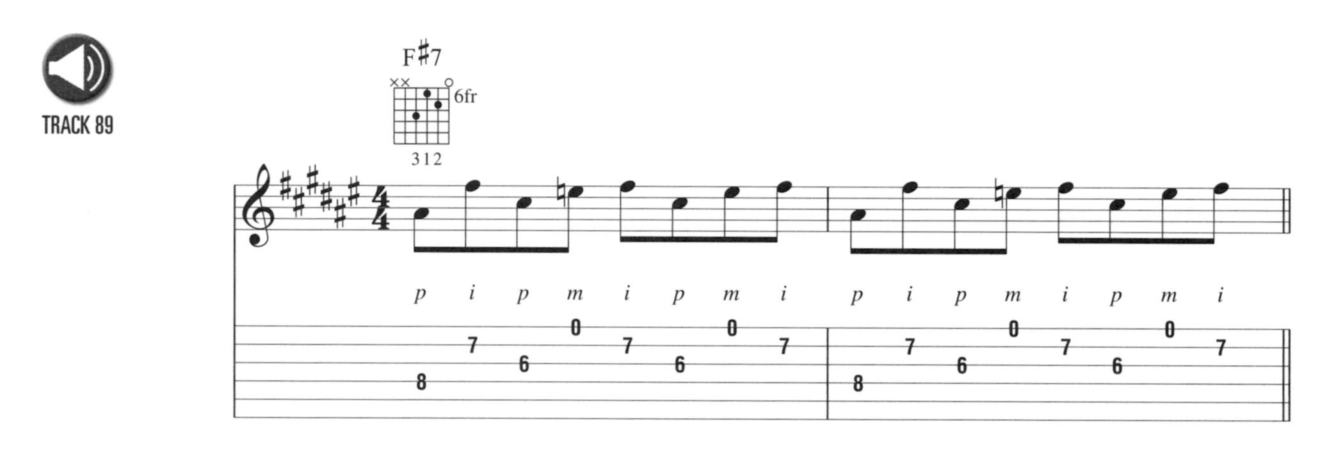

You might have noticed that all of these roll-pattern examples use *open strings*. Atkins was a big fan of using the open strings whenever possible—in picking patterns, roll patterns, and single-note runs. If he wanted to play a C major scale, for instance, he might play it like this, instead of fretting every note:

Here's another way Atkins might have approached playing a G major scale, coming down from the higher strings.

You could also play a similar G major scale pattern farther up the neck, like this:

TRACK 92

Atkins would incorporate these scales into his playing, but he'd also use the open strings in runs and fills, like this one, which is similar to a fill Atkins played while performing "Tiger Rag."

TRACK 93

He was also fond of playing pull-off runs at the nut that incorporated open strings, like this G run that is similar to what he played in a performance of "Sandman."

TRACK 94

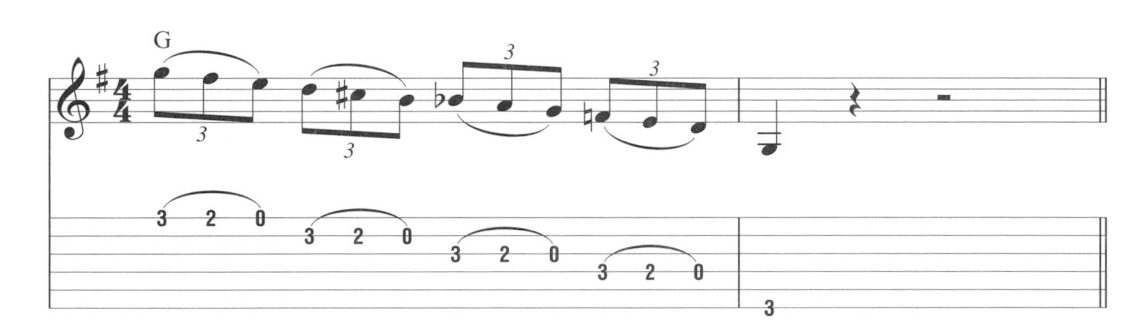

BASS TRICKS

Sometimes you might find yourself in a position where you can't reach an alternate-bass note with your thumb—like when you're playing up the neck while using most of your fingers for a melody line or when playing an unusual chord type. There are some tricks that Chet and others have used that can help you modify your bass line when this happens: one thing you can do is simply *omit a bass note* on occasion to accommodate a melody. For instance, the melody in this example slides way up to the 12th fret, then pops down to the 5th fret so you can grab the alternate-bass note on the fourth string again. But while we're briefly up high, we don't have as easy access to that bass note (we don't want to fret the fifth string at the 12th fret since it will dampen our low A bass note), so we can omit the second bass note in that measure, like this:

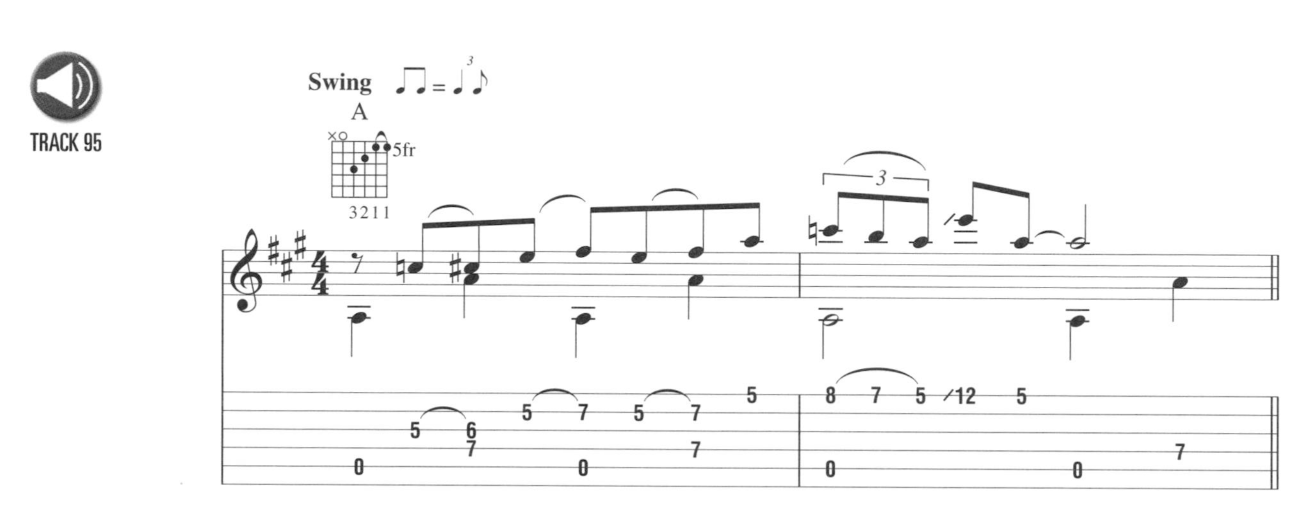

Another thing you could do is simply *play an open string*. Sometimes this moves by so quickly that you won't really notice that it's not part of the chord, and Chet used this trick often. Here we play the open D string in the bass while we slide up to the high note in the melody:

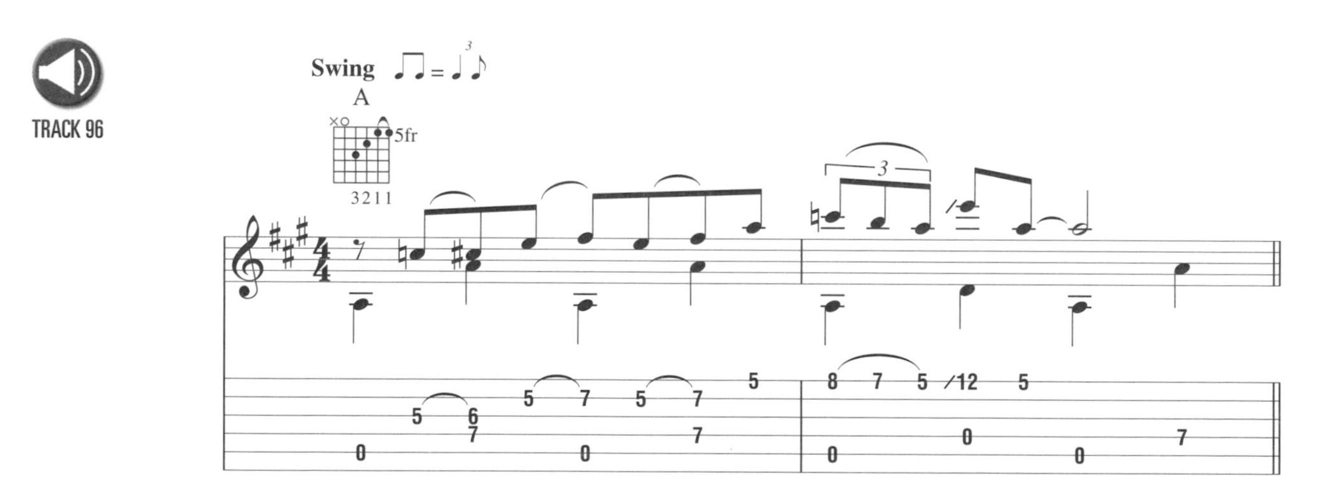

If you're not happy with the sound of that bass note, another thing you could try is *completely muting the note* while hitting the string. You won't hear a note, but the percussive, thumping sound you do get still helps drive the song forward. You can either mute it by using your picking hand to palm mute the string completely or by using your fret-hand fingers to mute the note.

TRACK 97

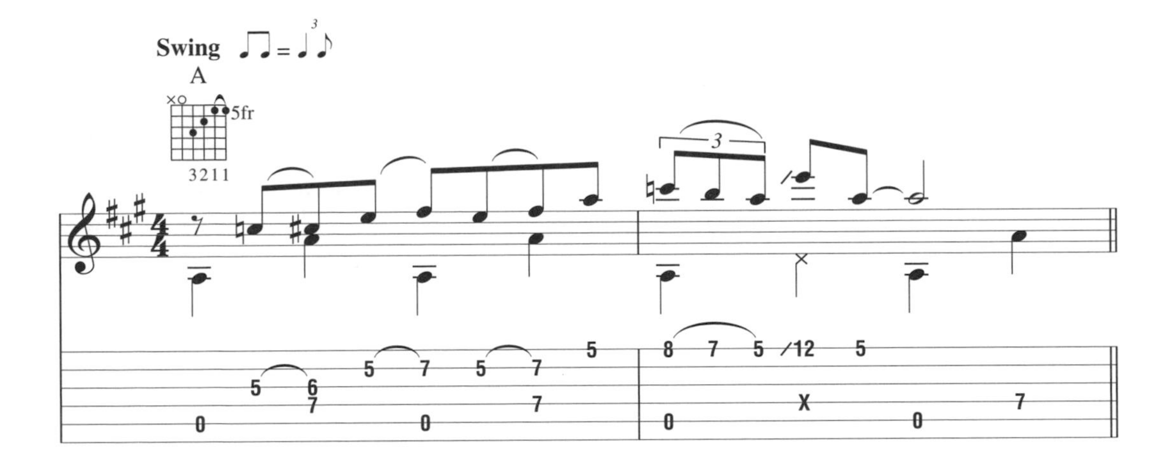

You'll rarely need to completely mute a note, however, like we did in the previous example. Usually, an open string passes by so quickly that it sounds fine. But when you really want to have a bass note that works with a chord, in most instances, you can rearrange your fingers on the fly to fret bass notes that work for a chord.

The following example in the key of B♭m shows this finger-twisting concept in action. The first measure is fairly straightforward. Start by barring your index finger across the top two strings for the B♭m chord and use your thumb on the bass note, then access the melody notes that move up the first string by using your pinky finger. At the beginning of the second measure, move your hand up the neck (but keep that thumb anchored on the bass note!) and play the first two melody notes with your middle and pinky fingers. Then reach down and grab the high bass note with your index finger before shifting your hand down to grab the C note with your middle finger. Finally, let your hand resume its original position for the second half of measure 2.

TRACK 98

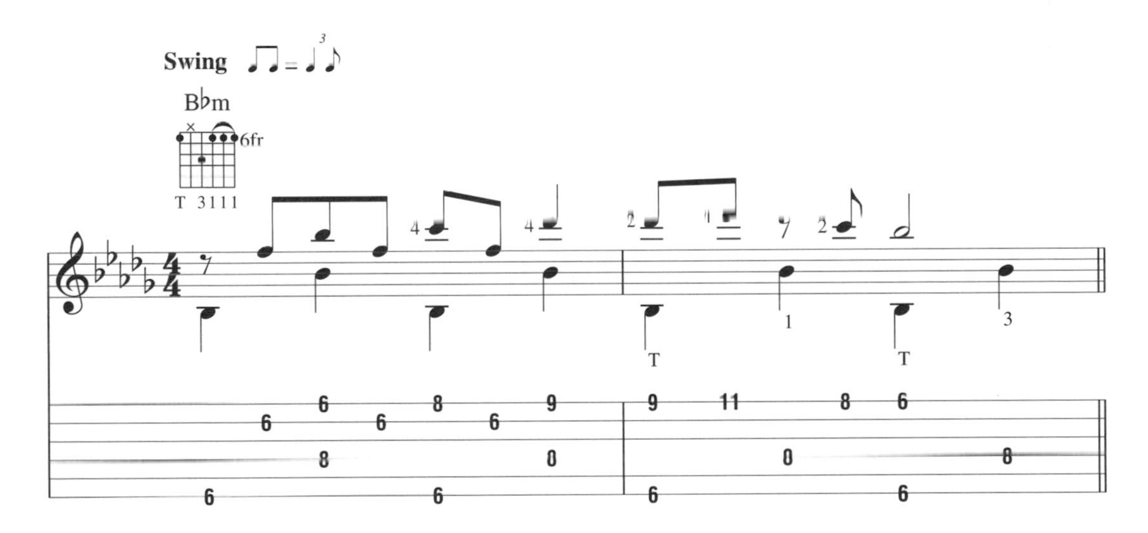

Playing in Alternate Tunings

As we've seen in this section, finding good bass notes under our melodies can sometimes be troublesome. In open and *alternate tunings*, the strings are often tuned to a chord, which makes finding bass notes easy. For instance, if you're tuned to *open D tuning* (low to high: D–A–D–F♯–A–D) and playing D chords, then all three of the low open strings will work as bass notes.

For those who aren't comfortable playing in heavily altered tunings, *drop D tuning* is a great place to start (low to high: D–A–D–G–B–E). Over a D chord, you can play all of the bottom three open strings as bass notes. Since only the bottom string is tuned down, all of your chord shapes will work on the top five strings. Also, when you're playing up the neck, a one-finger barre will transfer those bass notes to other chords.

CALM, COOL, AND COLLECTED

Now let's try a full song in the style of Chet Atkins. "Calm, Cool, and Collected" uses many of these techniques to emulate a classic Atkins sound found on songs like "Windy and Warm." The A section (the first eight measures) stays down at the nut of the guitar, then climbs up to fifth position for the B section at measure 10. Note the open-string scalar run in measure 4, and check out the bass trick in measures 6–7, where the open D string is used in place of the 2nd-fret E to make things easier to play—plus, it doesn't sound half bad!

TRACK 99

CALM, COOL, AND COLLECTED

Music by Andrew DuBrock

C7sus2
13111
F
T 3211
E
231
A
Am
231
E
231
Am
231
Am
5fr
134111

GUITAR NOTATION LEGEND

Guitar music can be notated three different ways: on a *musical staff*, in *tablature*, and in *rhythm slashes*.

RHYTHM SLASHES are written above the staff. Strum chords in the rhythm indicated. Use the chord diagrams found at the top of the first page of the transcription for the appropriate chord voicings. Round noteheads indicate single notes.

THE MUSICAL STAFF shows pitches and rhythms and is divided by bar lines into measures. Pitches are named after the first seven letters of the alphabet.

TABLATURE graphically represents the guitar fingerboard. Each horizontal line represents a string, and each number represents a fret.

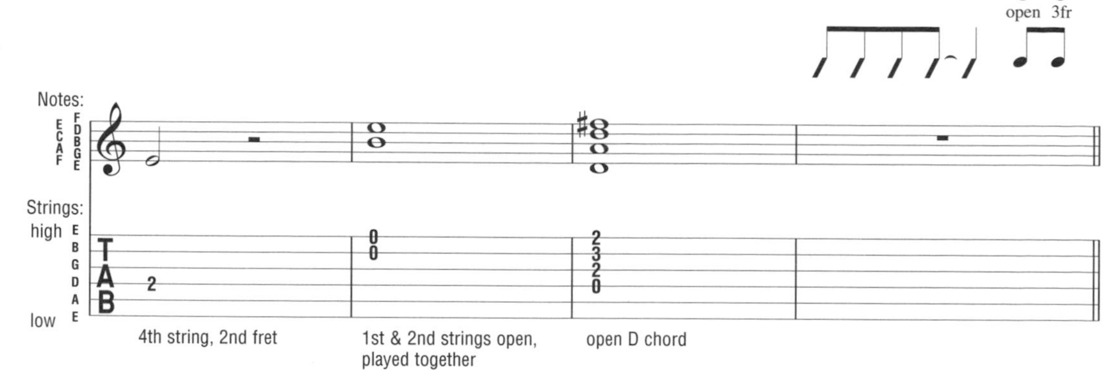

HALF-STEP BEND: Strike the note and bend up 1/2 step.

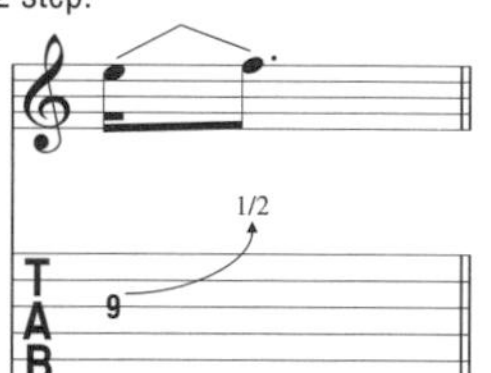

WHOLE-STEP BEND: Strike the note and bend up one step.

GRACE NOTE BEND: Strike the note and immediately bend up as indicated.

SLIGHT (MICROTONE) BEND: Strike the note and bend up 1/4 step.

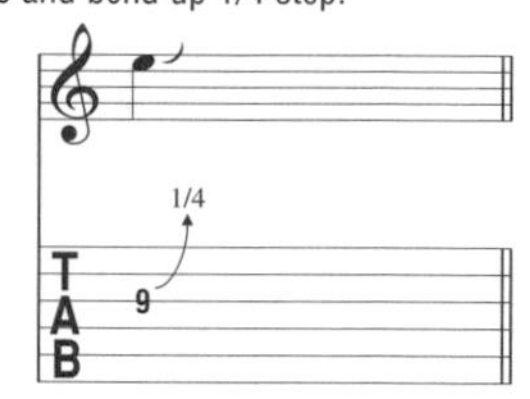

BEND AND RELEASE: Strike the note and bend up as indicated, then release back to the original note. Only the first note is struck.

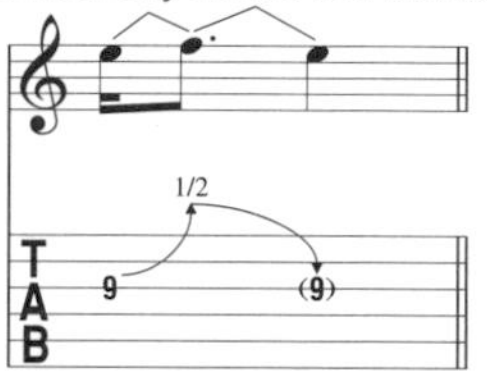

PRE-BEND: Bend the note as indicated, then strike it.

VIBRATO: The string is vibrated by rapidly bending and releasing the note with the fretting hand.

WIDE VIBRATO: The pitch is varied to a greater degree by vibrating with the fretting hand.

HAMMER-ON: Strike the first (lower) note with one finger, then sound the higher note (on the same string) with another finger by fretting it without picking.

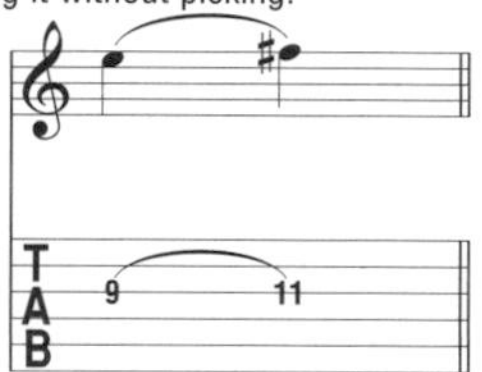

PULL-OFF: Place both fingers on the notes to be sounded. Strike the first note and without picking, pull the finger off to sound the second (lower) note.

LEGATO SLIDE: Strike the first note and then slide the same fret-hand finger up or down to the second note. The second note is not struck.

SHIFT SLIDE: Same as legato slide, except the second note is struck.

TRILL: Very rapidly alternate between the notes indicated by continuously hammering on and pulling off.

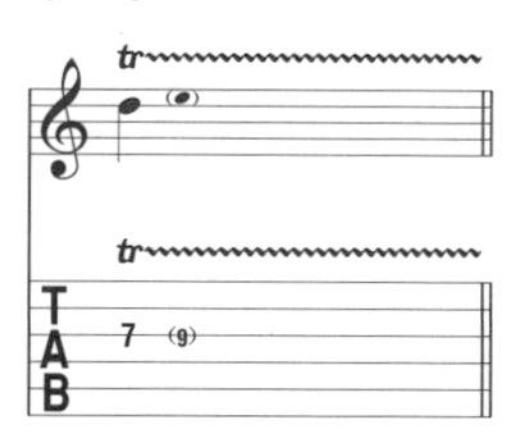

TAPPING: Hammer ("tap") the fret indicated with the pick-hand index or middle finger and pull off to the note fretted by the fret hand.

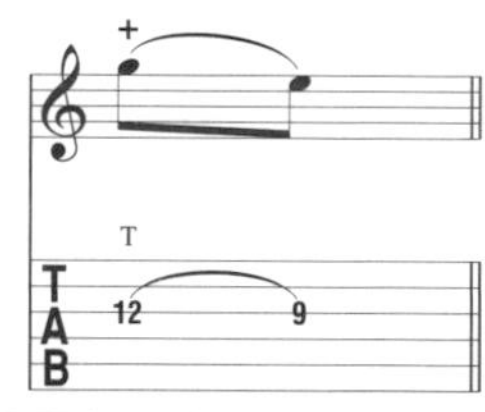

NATURAL HARMONIC: Strike the note while the fret-hand lightly touches the string directly over the fret indicated.

PINCH HARMONIC: The note is fretted normally and a harmonic is produced by adding the edge of the thumb or the tip of the index finger of the pick hand to the normal pick attack.

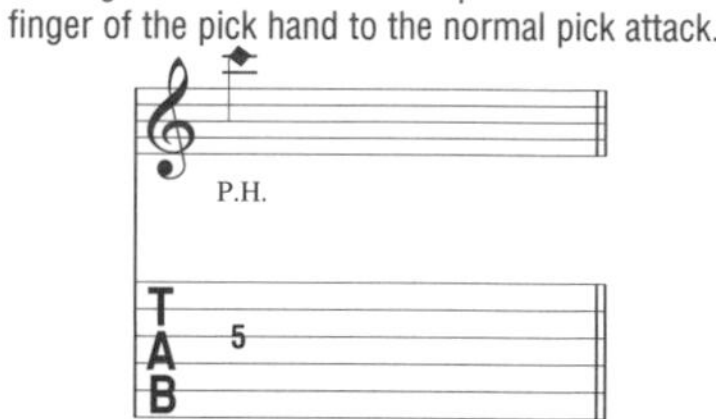

PICK SCRAPE: The edge of the pick is rubbed down (or up) the string, producing a scratchy sound.

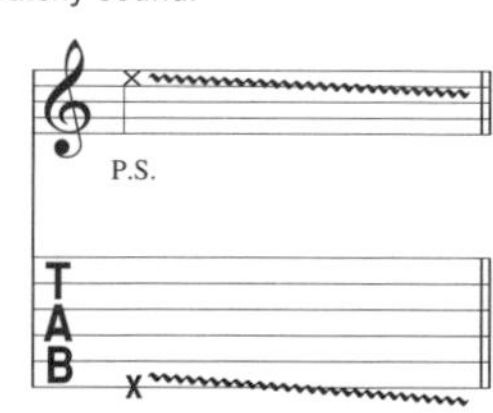

MUFFLED STRINGS: A percussive sound is produced by laying the fret hand across the string(s) without depressing, and striking them with the pick hand.

PALM MUTING: The note is partially muted by the pick hand lightly touching the string(s) just before the bridge.

RAKE: Drag the pick across the strings indicated with a single motion.

TREMOLO PICKING: The note is picked as rapidly and continuously as possible.

VIBRATO BAR DIVE AND RETURN: The pitch of the note or chord is dropped a specified number of steps (in rhythm), then returned to the original pitch.

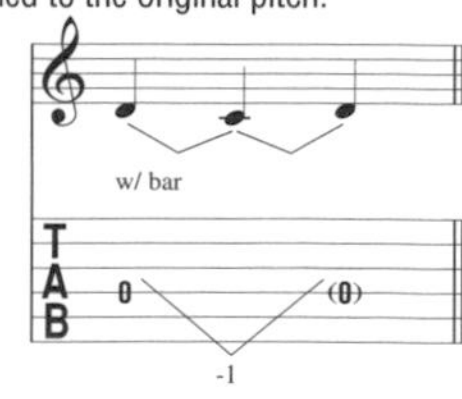

VIBRATO BAR SCOOP: Depress the bar just before striking the note, then quickly release the bar.

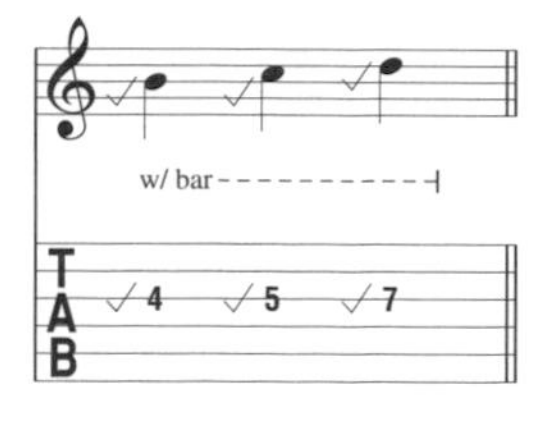

VIBRATO BAR DIP: Strike the note and then immediately drop a specified number of steps, then release back to the original pitch.

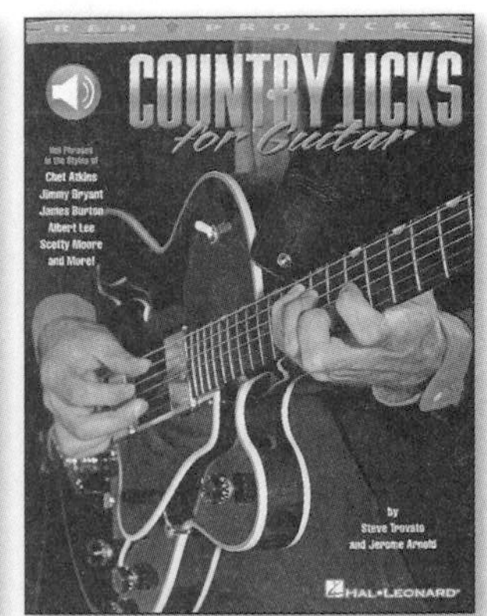

Guitar Instruction

Country Style!

from Hal Leonard

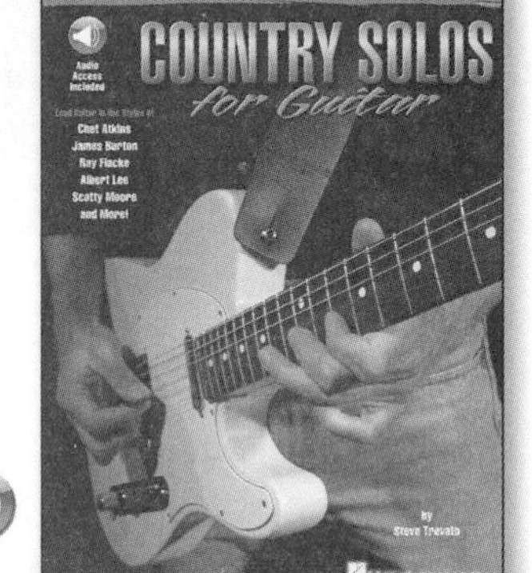

CHICKEN PICKIN' • *by Eric Halbig*

This book provides a "bird's-eye-view" of the techniques and licks common to playing hot, country lead guitar! Covers over 100 hot country guitar licks: open-string licks, double-stop licks, scales, string bending, repetitive sequences, and chromatic licks. The online audio includes 99 demonstration tracks with each lick performed at two tempos.

00695599 Book/Online Audio....................$17.99

DANIEL DONATO – THE NEW MASTER OF THE TELECASTER

Pathways to Dynamic Solos

This exclusive instructional book and DVD set includes guitar lessons taught by young Nashville phenom Daniel Donato. The "New Master of the Telecaster" shows you his unique "pathways" concept, opening your mind and fingers to uninhibited fretboard freedom, increased music theory comprehension, and more dynamic solos! The DVD features Daniel Donato himself providing full-band performances and a full hour of guitar lessons. The book includes guitar tab for all the DVD lessons and performances. Topics covered include: using chromatic notes • application of bends • double stops • analyzing different styles • and more. DVD running time: 1 hr., 4 min.

00121923 Book/DVD Pack....................$19.99

FRETBOARD ROADMAPS – COUNTRY GUITAR

The Essential Patterns That All the Pros Know and Use • by Fred Sokolow

This book/CD pack will teach you how to play lead and rhythm in the country style anywhere on the fretboard in any key. You'll play basic country progressions, boogie licks, steel licks, and other melodies and licks. You'll also learn a variety of lead guitar styles using moveable scale patterns, sliding scale patterns, chord-based licks, double-note licks, and more. The book features easy-to-follow diagrams and instructions for beginning, intermediate, and advanced players.

00695353 Book/CD Pack....................$16.99

HOW TO PLAY COUNTRY LEAD GUITAR

by Jeff Adams

Here is a comprehensive stylistic breakdown of country guitar techniques from the past 50 years. Drawing inspiration from the timelessly innovative licks of Merle Travis, Chet Atkins, Albert Lee, Vince Gill, Brent Mason and Brad Paisley, the near 90 musical examples within these pages will hone your left and right hands with technical string-bending and rolling licks while sharpening your knowledge of the thought process behind creating your own licks, and why and when to play them.

00131103 Book/Online Audio....................$19.99

COUNTRY LICKS FOR GUITAR

by Steve Trovato and Jerome Arnold

This unique package examines the lead guitar licks of the masters of country guitar, such as Chet Atkins, Jimmy Bryant, James Burton, Albert Lee, Scotty Moore, and many others! The online audio includes demonstrations of each lick at normal and slow speeds. The instruction covers single-string licks, pedal-steel licks, open-string licks, chord licks, rockabilly licks, funky country licks, tips on fingerings, phrasing, technique, theory, and application.

00695577 Book/Online Audo....................$19.99

COUNTRY SOLOS FOR GUITAR

by Steve Trovato

This unique book/audio pack lets guitarists examine the solo styles of axe masters such as Chet Atkins, James Burton, Ray Flacke, Albert Lee, Scotty Moore, Roy Nichols, Jerry Reed and others. It covers techniques including hot banjo rolls, funky double stops, pedal-steel licks, open-string licks and more, in standard notation and tab with phrase-by-phrase performance notes. The online audio includes full demonstrations and rhythm-only tracks.

00695448 Book/Online Audio....................$19.99

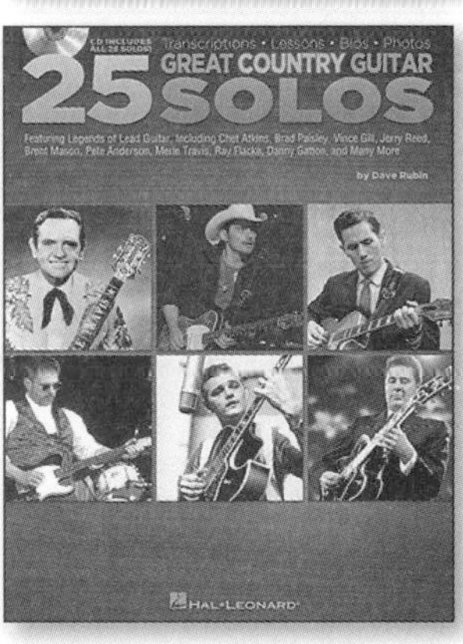

RED-HOT COUNTRY GUITAR

by Michael Hawley

The complete guide to playing lead guitar in the styles of Pete Anderson, Danny Gatton, Albert Lee, Brent Mason, and more. Includes loads of red-hot licks, techniques, solos, theory and more.

00695831 Book/Online Audio....................$19.99

25 GREAT COUNTRY GUITAR SOLOS

by Dave Rubin

Provides solo transcriptions in notes & tab, lessons on how to play them, guitarist bios, equipment notes, photos, history, and much more. The CD contains full-band demos of every solo in the book. Songs include: Country Boy • Foggy Mountain Special • Folsom Prison Blues • Hellecaster Theme • Hello Mary Lou • I've Got a Tiger by the Tail • The Only Daddy That Will Walk the Line • Please, Please Baby • Sugarfoot Rag • and more.

00699926 Book/CD Pack....................$19.99

www.halleonard.com

Prices, contents, and availability subject to change without notice.